THE
FEDERAL RESERVE
SCANDAL

THE
FEDERAL RESERVE
SCANDAL

Billy James Hargis
and
Bill Sampson

New Leaf
Press
Green Forest, AR 72638

First Edition

©Copyright, 1984
by New Leaf Press, Inc.
Green Forest, Arkansas 72638

Printed in the United States of America.

Library of Congress Number 84-061917
ISBN Number 0-89221-119-9

DEDICATION

TO: Mr. and Mrs. J. W. Seward, two great patriots whose loyalty to the Lord Jesus Christ has inspired them to be stalwart champions of free America.

TO: James J. Kelly, a man who has the deepest love for our God and country ideals, truly a kindly one in our world today.

TO: Mrs. C. C. Sugden, a patriot who is concerned about America free.

TO: Dedicated to Jimmy Hargis and Nesby Sampson, the fathers of the authors, men who knew the real value of a dollar because they had to work so hard for it.

Table of Contents

How This Book Helps

If you feel that somehow money has gotten out of control, that something of someone is cheating you about money, that inflation and rising prices and unemployment and politics and war are making money both worth less and worthless, then reading this book will tell you why...or at least may provide you with many answers.

This is a book about money but not a book about how to get rich. This is a book about banks and bankers but not an investment guide or a sales pitch for commodities of any kind. *This is a book that will help you get a grip on where you are in today's chaotic world economy.* It won't tell you how to make money or what to do with it when and if you have it.

What it will tell you is that putting trust in men cannot compare with putting trust in God, whether in money matters or anything else. What it will tell you is that with faith in God you need not fear men and their money or what they have done to ruin—except for an elite few—the world's economy.

"In God We Trust" is printed on the almost worthless coinage of our country. We say worthless because coins as they are minted today, are not worth their face value. They are fiat or phony money, too.

INTRODUCTION

How safe is your money?

It is as safe as you think it is. The more you research the subject of money, the less safe it seems to be. The more you *know* about money, its absolutely precarious position becomes apparent.

Money is predicated upon trust in men. The Holy Scripture, God's Word, tells us no man is perfect—no, not one. So our trust in money and men is imperfect, very fragile at best.

The best thing ever done about money was when the United States put the words "In God We Trust" on coins. We can't trust in the coins, despite those words, but we can trust in God. Because the Founding Fathers of this nation trusted in God instead of men, they devised a new kind of government on this earth, a government which divided the power of men who govern into three branches—the executive, the legislative and the judicial—all with Constitutionally equal power. This provided a series of checks and balances to prevent men who govern in this nation from becoming tyrants.

Had we remained true to the Constitution which our inspired forefathers wrote, we would not be in all the trouble we find ourselves and our country in today. Lack of vigilance, the unresisted erosion of liberty, the financial and political manipulation by dark powers, corruption, man's imperfection, greed, lust and sin—all contributed to the undermining and downfall of the Constitution and with it the faith in governing institutions which rested upon it.

The failure of these institutions, and many of the men who were and are the administrators of them, led the nation astray into domestic strife, surrenders of liberty, foreign entanglements and finally war—the most recent of which is still going on today.

9

The Final War

The United States has been in a big shooting, economic and political war with much of the rest of the world since 1917—the year we entered World War I and the year of the successful communist revolution in Russia.

There has never been any true peace since then for America or for the rest of the world. There have been "time outs," mistakenly called "peace," between rounds of the fight to allow exhausted participants to regain some strength, and then the fighting has resumed.

World War I was a time when modern technology entered into warfare on a large scale with the machine gun and tremendously high explosive artillery missiles. The carnage was unprecedented. Millions of men were killed in the ten square miles around Verdun alone. Millions more died at Somme, the British losing 20,000 in one battle there in 1916. Millions more died in other battles. The world never recovered from the losses. Satan rejoiced and took the opportunity to loose not only a temporary plague of influenza upon the world, but also a permanent plague of atheistic communism—the best method he has found yet to inflict pain and death upon mankind. Communism can be held responsible for another 142 million deaths since the Russian Revolution. There has never been a plague like it before or since in sheer numbers killed—not the Black Plague of Medieval times, not the worldwide influenza plague of World War I, nor the plague of the Axis and their holocausts of World War II.

The carnage of World War I, and the emergence of communism out of it as a dominant world force, changed the world as never before, and there is no turning back. It was as if the world that God created had officially ended and the rule of Satan had begun. Only a few salients, strongholds, of God's people remained: the United States and its allies—the remnants of the free world, of Western Civilization and Christianity. The rest of the world, the most of the world, and most of the other people in the world are under the domination of godless communism, or Satan, or other demonic "gods;" and their numbers and territory are increasing.

That's the background of this book about money and power in a world today where the only true hope is an acknowledgment of the sovereignty of Jesus Christ, the Saviour. All else is hopeless. Bible prophecy is quite clear on what will ultimately happen: *Jesus Christ will return and save His people.* The job God's people must do now is bring as many to Christ as possible before it is too late.

The Secret Conspiracy

Based on public records, it now seems to us that a secret conspiracy rules the world today—a conspiracy of international bankers who have financed the rise of communism at the expense of capitalism, in the mistaken belief they know more than anyone else and can manage the world better. In the final days, their empire will tumble down and they will perish.

The secret conspiracy was born of the carnage of World War I, rising like a specter out of the mud and blood of the trenches to rule over the doomed proceedings at Versailles in 1919 that sealed the old world's fate with a finality that only the nuclear age has made clear.

The Treaty of Versailles, supposedly "ending" World War I, in fact only perpetuated it by imposing upon a defeated and financially broken Germany impossible war reparations by which the victors expected the losers to pay all the infinite costs of the war. Germany already had spent everything it had fighting the war. It had nothing left to pay but the victors insisted upon payment.

The Germans were forced to turn to the richest country in the world, the United States, to "borrow" the money. Great Britain was nearly as broke as Germany, having wasted its treasure and a generation of young men on the war which also was to cost it its "old empire" in a few years. France had been the battleground and was destroyed physically and financially. The war also undermined the French colonial empire. Italy was helpless and poor even before the war. The communists who had taken over Russia were looting the slain Czar's treasures to keep their infant and very unstable revolution alive at the time. No one had any money to lend Germany except the United States—meaning the United States citizens who had been subjected to an inhuman income tax burden in 1913. World War I began the next year.

So, the United States was faced with the financially dismaying prospect of rebuilding Europe by "loaning" money to Germany so it could pay war reparations owed to our other allies—Great Britain, France, Italy and Japan. German bankers were handling massive amounts of money, skimming off what they could to rebuild German finance and passing the rest on to their conquerors while the German people suffered. This was the time in the 1920s that German marks were so worthless that it took a wheelbarrow full of them to buy a loaf of bread, if a loaf of bread could be found for sale. This was the kind of ruthless economics that gave rise to Hitler, who was among the first, and certainly the loudest, to proclaim that Germany should not have to pay the war reparations with money it did not have and could never repay.

The economic consequences of World War I lay behind America's stock market crash, the rise of the demonic Hitler, the Great Depression and World War II.

It was in the midst of this economic chaos that bankers from the United States and European countries began trying to bring their version of *order* to a world gone mad. After a dozen years of running a financial madhouse following World War I, climaxed with world depression brought on by the economic collapse of 1929, a coalition or cartel or "conspiracy," if you will, of European bankers persuaded their governments to call an economic summit meeting at the Hague, Netherlands. With the blessing, unofficial as it was, of the old League of Nations (to which

11

the U.S. never belonged) the bankers reached an agreement in 1930 which, among other things, established a superbank called the Bank for International Settlements—so named to settle the war reparations matter between Germany and the rest of the world. The bankers' agreement of 1930 came to be called "The Treaty of Hague", but it was not really a "treaty," only an indication that bankers had become governments with superman authority—in their own right.

It had become obvious to them, by that time, that Hitler was unfortunately right in saying Germany could not pay the reparations. Whether it should pay or not was beside the point. The fact was it could not pay, even with their millions of freshly-printed paper marks. All the reparation money Germany could ever pay, it received from the United States; and after the Wall Street crash of 1929 and the onset of the Depression, the U.S. could no longer underwrite the reparations or the financial operations of Europe.

The Bank for International Settlements, located in Basel, Switzerland, was created by the 1930 Hague agreement and is a major topic of this book. The BIS, as it is known, has effective control, if not outright ownership, of the Federal Reserve System of the United States, by holding in hock America's once vast gold horde, calling the shots for operation of the greater part of the world's economy (both capitalist and communist), and thus has become the most powerful institution in the world today, including the United States government. There is a lot to be said about the BIS, the Federal Reserve, and the men who created and control them and this book will attempt to say it.

The Basic Economic Mistake

A noted Texan made a basic economic mistake—he bought both guns and butter and went broke. The man was President Lyndon Johnson. The guns were for the Vietnam War. The butter (social spending) was for the so-called Great Society. Going broke is the legacy Johnson and several of his immediate predecessors left for our country...the United States of America.

Not all of America's economic problems can be blamed on Lyndon Johnson, but it was his foolhardy decision to have both guns and butter for too long that turned the American economy toward today's economic and monetary crisis.

Any student of economics knows that you can't have both guns and butter. That's basic knowledge in any economics course. It's common sense. You can have more of one than the other, but you can't have both in abundant, equal amounts. You must sacrifice some of one to have a sufficient amount of the other. Economists call this sacrifice "opportunity cost"—meaning if you spend your money on one thing, it has cost you the opportunity to spend it on something else. This is the kind of choice people must make daily to live. The only way to spend for both is to over-extend your credit until you are broke. That's the decision President "LBJ" made for America in the mistaken notion that somehow "government" is different from "people" and immune from their problems. He and other politicians of like mind always forget that "government" IS the people.

Johnson tried to pay for both the escalating war in Vietnam and the rising costs of Great Society social programs—some of which he had inherited from John Kennedy and some of which he developed on his own.

Johnson was a product of the "tax big and spend big" school of political thought based on the government intervention theories of the British economist, John Maynard Keynes. Keynes books, *Treatise on Money* (1930) and *General Theory of Employment, Interest and Money* (1936), provided guidelines for President Franklin D. Roosevelt's "brain trust" of advisers who planned the "New Deal" in an effort to get America out of the depression of the 1930's. The plan, basically, was to spend "government money"—that is, the people's tax money—in unprecedented amounts for social programs and civic projects. It didn't work. The depression continued until World War II when record spending by several countries, including Great Britain, for the war effort (spending of much money which simply did not exist) began flooding the American economy with what amounted to phony money, or "fiat" money as it is known ("fiat" being a Latin word much like the English word "faith.") Money based on faith is only as good as you believe it is. Fiat money or phony money is paper money declared to be legal tender by law, although not backed by gold or silver and not necessarily redeemable in coin. This was the phony, make-believe stuff of Keynes' theory of economics.

The rationale for creating this money was "What difference does it make? We only owe it to ourselves." But the truth is that we don't owe it to ourselves. *We owe it to someone else who holds the power of the papers, the U.S. bonds, on which the money is based.* Now the party is over and the piper must be paid. The bill has come due on an unprecedented world-wide scale and there is no money to pay it. There is only the paper money, the fiat money, the phony money.

The Lost Gamble

Nations that are in debt—and that means all of them—the entire world—face a massive default. America's debt is far more than $1 trillion and growing. There is no serious thought being given to ever paying it off, only increasing it. What about the prosperous countries like Japan, Singapore, Switzerland, Hong Kong, and the Arab lands? They are not as prosperous as they appear on paper when their economies are analyzed and their debts totaled up. Some of them are only the momentary holders of fiat money—poker chips as it were—in the world economic gambling game. The real question is where are they going to cash them in? There is no place...no pay window. This phony money just continues to circulate in ever-increasing amounts, becoming worth less and less as it goes.

The Arabs, for example, put their assumed riches from oil in London, New York, Paris and Swiss banks. They dare not keep it in their politically unstable and war-torn Middle East. The banks know that money idle in a vault is worthless, so they speculate with it. That is, they gamble, by loaning it out in massive amounts to so-called "Developing Countries" (which are in fact "Less Developed Countries" or LDCs of the "Third World" or new countries created from old colonial systems) and to communist countries.

Ruth Sheldon Knowles, the oil consultant, once wrote a book called *The Greatest Gamblers* about oilmen who risk high stakes on drilling wildcat wells on the chance they may hit it rich with an oil strike. They are pikers compared with the international bankers who have gambled and lost on "Third World" and communist countries ever becoming economically strong enough to repay the massive loans made to them by the big gambling bankers.

It is these bankers who "own" or control America's economy because they privately own America's central bank known as the Federal Reserve System, which issues all America's money. The Federal Reserve System is not a "federal" or a government bank any more than the Bank of England is "owned" by the English government or the crown. The Federal Reserve and the Bank of England are merely deceptive names used by financiers to give dignity to these institutions representing banking.

Who Can You Trust

We wrote this book with two things mind: to explain how America and the world got into the financial crisis it is in today and to show that Jesus Christ, not men or their money, is still the only hope of the world.

We'll take a look at the BIS and the Federal Reserve, certainly; but also, we will examine such things as money itself, big banks and bankers, currency and the pathetic attempts puny man has made to "control" it, capitalism, some ideals of American government and free enterprise, communism and its relation to Satan, what the United Nations is really all about when it comes to money and economics and world trade, and the meaning of gold and silver as basic foundations for money.

All this is not as serious as it sounds because all of it is folly, and all of it shall pass away in the end without a trace or memory or history, when Jesus returns. Meanwhile, we must live with it in a world of greed, corruption and evil. Christians have a responsibility to prepare for the Saviour's return, to bring as many to Him as possible, to live their own caring lives as He instructed and, as He said, "to render unto Caesar those things which are Ceasar's and unto God those which are God's."

This is why it is important for Christians to know about the world in which they live, about Caesar's things as well as God's, so they can tell the difference; about evil as well as good, so they can make the correct choice; and about Satan, his demons and his many snares and disguises, so they can be avoided.

Money certainly is important to survival, even in this sinful world; and everyone needs it, both believer and unbeliever. But the difference between the believer and the unbeliever is that the believer has faith in God and in God's Word—the Holy Bible—which says that God will provide for His own—the faithful. The unbeliever has only himself upon which to rely for deliverance, or whatever other "god" he has put his faith in (which too often is money, not evil in itself but the root of all evil).

We are convinced that upon reading this book, you will be much better informed about Christian survival in an evil world that has come to be dominated by money—a tool that Satan can use effectively but it's not nearly as effective as God's power. Money is neither good nor evil in itself. Those who use it, who spend it and save it and invest it, are the ones who decide the fate and consequences of money—the ones who decide whether its use will be for the profane or the sacred.

Chapter 1

POWER OF THE PURSE STRING
The Case of Vanishing Gold

The most powerful bank in the world has twenty miles of underground vaults tunneled into solid rock and holding most of the world's gold supply, including what used to be the United States' bonanza treasure from the California Gold Rush and the Klondike.

What used to be America's gold was drained off through the so-called "London Gold Pool," an agency of the world's most powerful bank, in the 1960s to pay for the guns of Vietnam and the political butter at home which buys votes provided by the Kennedy and Johnson administrations.

The former American-owned gold is lodged deeply in the underground vaults of the Bank for International Settlements, Basel, Switzerland, the most powerful bank in the world. Americans still like to think the gold is in Fort Knox, Kentucky, but no president since Franklin D. Roosevelt has personally seen any of the gold in Fort Knox and, in fact, Roosevelt didn't see all of it. President Ronald Reagan appointed a seventeen-member gold commission to investigate the possibility of putting America back on the gold standard; but the commission's efforts to audit the gold in Fort Knox has been stonewalled at every turn by the Federal Reserve, a virtual agency of the Bank for International Settlements, and the Federal Reserve's adjunct, the U.S. Treasury Department.

They don't want any American president or anyone else to look into the Fort Knox gold scandal because they and their predecessors have been accomplices in the biggest theft in the history of the world—the removal of tons of gold from Fort Knox and other U.S. bullion storehouses. The gold was transferred through the London Gold Pool to the vaults of the Bank for International Settlements, with vast amounts of paper credit based on the gold, going to Soviet Russia to build the world's mightiest anti-American military machine. Some $80 billion in gold vanished from America, financed Soviet credit, and then was stored in what are believed to be the safest vaults in the world, the twenty miles of tunnels in solid rock beneath the Alps in historically "neutral" Switzerland[1].

We're talking about 14,000 tons of gold!

The United States had more gold than any country in the world after World War II, some 700 million ounces, most of it stored in Fort Knox. Today, no one, except perhaps the head of the Federal Reserve, knows how much is left in Fort Knox, if any. Much of it apparently has been moved to the world's most powerful bank in Switzerland, a bank owned and controlled by a cartel or cabal or conspiracy—call it what you like—of powerful international bankers beyond the control of any government. The Bank for International Settlements is a government of its own.

No one outside the employment of the U.S. Treasury, which has become little more than a sub-agency of the private Federal Reserve owned by the bankers of the Bank for International Settlements, has seen any gold in Fort Knox since Roosevelt peeked at it in the 1930s to satisfy himself that the country could finance World War II, starting with lend-lease to Great Britian. Back in 1974, Fort Knox custodians showed some gold, or something that appeared to be gold, to six Congressmen and about 100 newsmen. They were allowed to look into one vault out of thirteen small ones on the upper level of Fort Knox. They were not allowed into the huge subterranean level where most of the gold is supposedly stored. The gold, if that's what it was, that they saw there was only showcase gold, or it could have been gold bricks—bricks with a veneer of gold. They certainly were not allowed to take bore samples. A Fort Knox official shaved off a few thin peelings of gold and had it assayed there for the benefit of the politicians and newsmen. Certainly that was gold, which for all intents satisfied Congress, the news media and, supposedly, the public given the report of the "gold investigation."[2]

The loss of America's gold, the continual inflationary monetary policies of the Federal Reserve and the now acceptable child-like faith of the American people in the "credit" of the government that backs the currency would explain why America's economy is in jeopardy.

The hard truth is this: America no longer is in control of its economic destiny no matter what any politicians in Washington, D.C., may say to the public through the news media.

The economic control of America and the rest of the world seems to be in the hands of the most powerful bank in the world, the Bank for International Settlements in Basel, Switzerland. It is systematically looting America through our national debt, our negative foreign trade balance and control of the Federal Reserve, which has a grip on the U.S. Treasury—the American tax collector and the actual printer of money.

This superbank and the bankers who run it decide who in the world gets money and who doesn't. They decide who succeeds and who fails, who wins and who loses. Local banks do the same thing with their selective loan policies.

The Story of the Superbank

To understand American economy and foreign policy, the Federal Reserve, and the often purely threatrical antics of Congress and presidents, when it comes to the U.S. budget, the federal deficit and the national debt, it is necessary to know something about the Bank for International Settlements, the world's superbank.

The European victors of World War I imposed the unrealistic Treaty of Versailles on defeated Germany in 1919, requiring Germany to pay war reparations for the loss of life and property by the victors in subduing the Germans. This caused Germany to borrow from America so it could pay England, France, Italy, Japan and other victors for the war. Such financial shenanigans led directly to the collapse of world trade and the stock market in the 1929-32 period and brought on the Great Depression.

Two important by-products resulted from the irrational demand by the victorious European allies who imposed a war reparations payment of 320 billion gold marks on a defeated and financially exhausted Germany: one was the creation of the Bank for International Settlements to find a realistic way for Germany to make some kind of reparations payments in accordance with the treaty of Versailles, and the other was the rise of Adolf Hitler whose nationalistic protests against reparations and other terms of the treaty eventually elevated him to the chancellorship and/or dictator of Germany in 1933.

The Bank for International Settlements was created by a series of economic planning conferences in Brussels, 1920; London, 1924; Brussels again 1927; and the Hague, Netherlands, 1929 and 1930. The reports of these conferences were reviewed and approved by the annual Council and Assembly meetings of the League of Nations in Geneva.[3]

The Reparations Commission of the League of Nations appointed a committee to draft recommendations for settling the German reparations issue posed by the Treaty of Versailles in as realistic manner as possible. This committee was headed by General Charles Dawes, American ambassador to England at the time (although the United States was not a member of the League of Nations, the U.S. was the major source of finance for reconstruction of Germany and the rest of Europe after the war and could not ignore its growing financial commitment); American corporate executive Owen D. Young of General Electric; Sir Arthur Salter of England, league Secretariat and his French assistant, Jean Monnet, later to be known as the "father" of the European Common Market; Aristide Briand, former French Prime Minister and Foreign Minister; heads of the European central banks and a number of their assistants and technicians, and a variety of economic experts.

Briand, incidentally, was a fervent promoter of what he called "The United States of Europe," and he often talked and wrote at length about a "new world economic order" and a "one-world government" he envisioned eventually evolving from the League of Nations. The United Nations is closer to Briand's dream than the League ever was, and it is still seen by one-worlders today as the vehicle for a new economic order and world government.

They were probably as good an assemblage of brains as could be gathered to face the reparations problem, and they became known simply as "The Experts" in both the press of that time and in later historical literature.[4]

Their plan was two-fold: (1) put the German economy back on its feet with massive loans and thus stabilize its currency and (2) extract funds from the revived German economy through railroad bonds, industrial bonds and taxation to pay a more modified and reasonable form of reparations.

It was the second point—how to get the reparations money out of Germany and distributed to the victorious governments who were signatories of the Treaty of Versailles—that led to the series of economic conferences which defined the need for a major international bank beyond control of any one government. The "Experts" meeting in 1929 put the finishing touches on the plan for the Bank for International Settlements, and it was formally approved by the Hague Agreements or Hague Treaty of 1930.

The bank was not just a creation of the League of Nations, which it survived, but of the more independent "experts" of the committee serving the League's Reparations Commission. It had a life of its own apart from the League and was financed by America, meaning American taxpayers and investors and banks and the banks' depositors. Although America was involved in the bank—in fact, its largest "depositor," if that's the word for the massive loans made through it to make German reparations payments possible—the Europeans did not consider it quite proper for Americans to be on the bank's board of governors since America was not a member of the League of Nations.

It was the old story of taxation without representation again but the American international financiers involved were not concerned about such political aspects as were the Patriots of 1776.

The frightened politicians of the League of Nations, who were as afraid of the political consequences of a financial collapse as they later would be of Hitler and Mussolini, bowed to the superbankers, dared not try to exert any control over them and did whatever they believed necessary at the time to retain office, popularity at home and whatever it was they perceived as political power.

Isolationist politicians in the U.S. Congress refused to sanction American participation in the Hague Conference and Treaty; but because the Federal Reserve was not beholden to Congress or the president or anyone, its chairman attended the conference, observed the treaty signing and became an ex-officio member of the bank's board—a post still held today.

The bankers came up with the plan for a world central bank, the superbank, and agreed to operate it to keep world economy on an even keel (they said) for a price—no government interference and no taxes.[5]

Hitler Became Their Created Hero

The deal was agreed upon and the Treaty of Hague of 1930 established the Bank for International Settlements. Its first order of business was to facilitate the reparations matter so it could get on with reconstruction of a new world economic order. The settlement of reparations, which in effect negated major sections of the Treaty of Versailles and relieved Germany of much of the financial obligations imposed upon it, helped make Hitler a national hero. He had been saying throughout the 1920s that the reparations were unfair and that Germany should refuse to pay them. When the superbankers did just what he was claiming should be done, it gave him a respectability he had never known and elevated him into German politics on the highest national level. He was chancellor within little over two years from the creation of the big bank and within another year was dictator. The bank's manipulations of world economics made it possible for the refinancing of German industrialists and the building of the military machine necessary for Hitler's Satanic power and heartless aggression leading to World War II.

While the people of the world divided up politically to fight World War II, the Bank for International Settlements maintained business as usual on an international scale, dealing with both Allies and Axis where a buck was to be made. Hitler looted gold from conquered nations and sent it to the bank for financial credits to keep his war machine running. The United States financed not only its "arsenal of democracy" but kept afloat the economy of Great Britain through various economic machinations engineered by the Federal Reserve through the big bank in Switzerland. To the bankers there, stolen European gold or California gold from America was all the same. A considerable amount of allied gold and money found its way to the United States to pay for armaments and some went to the big bank. American credit at that time was "good as gold" to international bankers because of the government's access to each American's income through taxation.

By 1944 it was obvious the Allies were going to defeat Germany and Japan and Italy. The idealistic pinned great hopes on creation of a United Nations dominated by the victors to maintain world peace. But the realistic planned a world economy to be dominated by the financial elite to maintain world control. Even before the war was over, the financial planners met at Bretton Woods, New Hampshire, to establish an International Monetary Fund and a World Bank, both to be agencies of the forthcoming United Nations.

Communists Plan The Future

A few naive Americans at the Bretton Woods meeting attempted to pass a resolution that would dismember the Bank for International Settlements and turn its duties to the new IMF and World Bank. They didn't know then that the Bretton Woods meeting was controlled by a communist agent working for the U.S. Secretary of Treasury and by a British sexual deviate whose now discredited economic ideas would both plunge the globe into deeper financial distress and toward World War III.

The communist agent was Harry Dexter White, who was personal representative of Secretary of the Treasurer Henry Morgenthau and who had the complete trust of President Roosevelt. The British pervert was John Maynard Keynes who thought something could be produced from nothing if enough people could be convinced that that "Big Lie" was true.[6]

White and Keynes led the attack against the American resolution to destroy the Bank for International Settlements. The reason is clear but sinister: the Big Bank was needed not just for an international financial clearinghouse—the World Bank could do that—but it was useful to govern without consent of the governed because it was beyond political control under terms of the Hague Treaty.

Beyond political control! Think of it! The Rothschilds, among the earliest of modern international bankers, held to the credo that whoever controls the money, rules. The big bank made it possible to rule without the inconvenience of obtaining political approval from those to be ruled. Control of the world's money and economy meant control of the world's destiny.

The United Nations, the International Monetary Fund, the World Bank—all showcase stuff for politicians. The big bank, the central bank of the world, would call the shots.

The Bank for International Settlements made a profit of $162 million in 1982, a modest enough figure for handling billions of dollars annually for the world's central banks. But it is not so much profit that interests the bankers who control the big bank as it is power. Any banker can make profits without hardly trying; but power—world power—that's something else.

One might wonder why nations' central banks, including the Federal Reserve in the United States, would want the BIS to handle investments and other financial transactions for them when they have huge trained staffs of people to do it themselves. The answer is...*secrecy*. Money "deposited" or "invested" in the Bank for International Settlements is not only secure as it would be anywhere else in the world, it can be used for ANYTHING without having to explain to the public, Congress, presidents, parliaments, monarchs, dictators, stockholders, boards of directors or anyone what it is being used for. The Bank for International Settlements provides the *most secret* of secret Swiss bank accounts—the secret financial manipulations of world nations.

Herein lies the explanation of how the capitalists are supplying the communists with enough rope for the communists to hang them, just as Marx said. Here is the way the wealth of the capitalist free nations can be transferred to communist nations and their Third World allies.

Herein also may lie the explanation of who "owns" the private money-currency issuing central bank of the United States known as the Federal Reserve, which will be discussed in detail in a subsequent chapter. It will suffice to say now that the Federal Reserve is little more than an arm of the Bank for International Settlements, the Fed having been instrumental along with the U.S. Treasury in selling out America's gold through the London Gold Pool to the Bank for International Settlements. When BIS was created in accordance with the 1930 Hague Treaty, a conspiratorial act of subterfuge was required to bring the Fed under control of the BIS. Because Congress could not and would not officially participate in organization of BIS, certain shares in the superbank were placed in trust with First National City Bank of New York in the Federal Reserve's name, which not only made Federal Reserve an "owner" of the Bank for International Settlements but also subjugated it to the majority decisions of the BIS board, of which the Fed was not a member.

The chairman of the Federal Reserve went to Basel, Switzerland, for the organizational meeting of the BIS and all Fed chairmen since then have attended the regular BIS board meetings, now held ten times each year.[7]

Rise of the American Comrade

The deep communist influence in the Federal Reserve in those early years of the Bank for International Settlements can be illustrated by the following story:

When "Comrade" Armand Hammer, president of Occidental Petroleum Co. of Los Angeles, was a young man, he smuggled contraband supplies from the United States into communist Russia before the U.S. formally extended diplomatic recognition to the Soviet Union in 1933. Hammer was rewarded by being paid in art treasures of the late Czar Nicholas Romanov, whom the communists had overthrown and killed along with his family. The communists stole the czar's treasures and turned them over to Hammer in return for services rendered to the communist cause.

To turn the treasures into cash, Hammer solicited big U.S. department stores to sell the stolen goods for him to the American public. One of the largest of these middlemen was Macy's Department Store in New York, which sold a considerable amount of the boodle (jewels, tapestries, furniture, religious icons, the special Fabrege collection, royal clothing and the like) to the Rockefeller family in New York.[8]

A Macy executive at the time who was instrumental in the deal was Beardsley Ruml, who also was chairman of the board of the Federal Reserve Bank in New York, the most important of the twelve Federal Reserve "branches" in the United States. There is no public record of how much money changed hands or who profited the most in these stolen goods transactions, but certainly Hammer made money as the originator of the blood-stained bargain, and Ruml profited as Macy's middleman to the Rockefellers.

Injecting The Tax Siphon

Ruml, linked to the Bank for International Settlements through his Federal Reserve position, hatched a plan at the outset of World War II to impose a "pay as you go" taxation program on American taxpayers that is now known as "withholding tax" or collecting taxes at the source. The scheme was sold to the Congress and the American public as "patriotic" to help pay for the war effort, but in reality it was a siphon tapped into the financial bloodstream of the American worker to drain off funds being produced by the American economy into the international bank through the Treasury-Federal Reserve arrangement.[9]

The Ruml withholding plan supposedly would strengthen the government in its critical fight against inflation by withdrawing puchasing power from the spending stream before it could exert an upward pressure on prices...and incidentally guarantee a more prompt and certain flow of revenue to the Treasury (and the Federal Reserve and the Bank for International Settlements) than the method of paying the entire tax amount owed annually. President Roosevelt endorsed the plan in his budget message of Janaury 6, 1943, as the withholding bill was working its way through Congress.

Conservative congressmen assailed the Ruml tax withholding plan as a scheme that would put middle class taxpayers into *hock* for life while providing high income taxpayers a one-year free ride on taxes. They said it would tax the heaviest those least able to pay such an economic sacrifice and excuse those most able to pay. Statistics introduced in Congress showed that some sixty millionaires then on the tax rolls would benefit to the tune of $854,000 each, while the low and middle income taxpayers would shoulder most of the tax burden. For example, one Congressman figured that the average millionaire's chauffeur would have to pay $1.87 in taxes while the millionaire himself was forgiven the $854,000.

The late Oklahoma Congressman Wesley Disney argued that the Ruml plan was a redistribution of the tax burden from the few to the many...in direct violation of the just and fundamental principle of ability to pay. He named names and made public tax statistics, charging that Charles Marcus of the Bendix Co. would pay only $177 in taxes on a 1942 war business income of $77,000; that J. D. Morrow of Joy Manufacturing would pay only $282 on an income of $55,000 and that J. W. Frazier of the Willys-Overland Co. (manufacturing Jeeps for the war effort) would pay $477 on $123,000 income.[10]

But the New Deal was still riding high in wartime Washington, and the Ruml plan for withholding passed the House 230 to 180 and the Senate 49 to 30. With only a few minor revisions in the House-Senate Conference Committee, it was signed into law by President Roosevelt on June 9, 1943, under the name Current Tax Payment Act of 1943.

The master plan of international bankers to directly tap the American taxpayer before he could ever get his hands on money he had earned was complete, having begun with the passage of the Federal Reserve Act and the 16th Amendment to the Constitution (the Income Tax Amendment), both in 1913. The creation of the Bank for International Settlements in 1930 established a world central bank for all national central banks, including the Federal reserve, and the Current Tax Payment Act of 1943 (withholding tax) injected the drain into the financial bloodstream of the American working man and woman who pay taxes into an international system where the money can be spent secretly and without democratic representation, to say nothing of republic organization.

The withholding tax plan was the brainstorm of Beardsley Ruml of the Fed and of Macy's, a close friend of Comrade Armand Hammer, who is allegedly the communists' most used and trusted ally in America. The best customer of the Kremlin-Hammer-Macy-Ruml conspiracy to dispose of the wealth taken from the murdered czar was the Rockefellers, with financial interests not only in Chase Manhattan Bank but also in the other banks and investment firms that privately own the Federal Reserve Bank, the American branch of the Bank for International Settlements. As we shall see in our chapter on the Federal Reserve, the U.S. Treasury prints government bonds to give to the Federal Reserve— yes, give—in return for printing the Federal Reserve notes used as currency in the United States. By this incredible method, the U.S. Treasury is, in fact, owned by the Federal Reserve; and the Federal Reserve, in turn, is owned by the international bankers controlling the Bank for International Settlements. So the United States' economy and currency are backed not by the highly-publicized "faith and credit" of the U.S. government, but by the whim of an international banking cartel holding the BIS.

Why Volker Triumphed

These facts and circumstances may help explain why President Reagan reappointed Paul Volker as chairman of the Federal Reserve Board in 1983. It had nothing to do with political ideology, the president being a political conservative in most matters and Volker being a liberal. It had to do with money, plain and simple. Volker was the Bank for International Settlements' choice to head the Fed, even when he was first "appointed" by President Jimmy Carter. The choice was probably not Carter's nor Reagan's, but the decision was made by the BIS, which holds the power of pursestring to America's gold, America's trillion dollar-plus debt, America's annual multi-billion dollar federal deficit. The one who pays the piper calls the tune, and in this case the BIS is financing the American economy much as it is the rest of the world, and so it names the Fed chairman. Volker is the big bankers' man and the publicity about Reagan possibly appointing a fiscal conservative to succeed Volker was just so much news media hype put out to fool the American public into thinking that the president actually had a choice when, in fact, he had none. The public speculation about Volker and the Fed setting higher or lower interest rates and requiring more or less money to be held in reserve by banks in order to tighten or loosen the money supply is so much more *media hype*. The shots are called by the Bank for International Settlements and only announced by Volker and the Fed as though they were his and the board's decisions.

America's money and economy has been *internationalized* through the Federal Reserve branch of the Bank for International Settlements. It may still look like American money, but that is merely illusion and not substance. The value of the dollar long ago quit being dependent upon American productivity and now is worth what the Bank for International Settlements says it is worth in international markets. This international financial trap into which America has fallen is far more sinister and deadly than George Washington ever dreamed when he warned the people of the United States to avoid entangling foreign alliances. Were it only not too late to heed his good advice!

Inside the Superbank

Just who does "own" the BIS and who is the big boss there who holds the destiny of nations, including the United States of America, in his hands? Such a powerful, evil man has been closely protected from publicity and other harm. It really makes little difference who he is because, no matter who occupies the office, his successor will be just like him as no man attains that position without complete approval of, without being the creation of, the international bankers who own him and the BIS. At this writing, the "president" of the Bank for International Settlements is Dr. Fritz Leutwiler, who also happens to be president of the Swiss National Bank, the only privately-owned central national bank except the Bank of England and the Federal Reserve, which is not represented on the BIS board. All other central national banks represented on the BIS board are government owned. To be government owned means to be answerable to the people or their representatives in the forms of presidents, parliaments, congresses, diets, knessets or whatever "democratic" institutions are used by governments ruling people. That's why central national banks have joined together to "own" and be owned in return by the superbank, the Bank for International Settlements. *They are free from democratic control and can do as they please.*

This big superbank is organized at three levels:

1. The board of directors represents the eight European central banks that own and are owned by the BIS: the central national banks of England, Switzerland, Germany, Italy, France, Belgium, Sweden and the Netherlands. The United States, through the Federal Reserve, is informally considered an "ex-officio member," a sort of bank without portfolio, invited to attend certain meetings at various executive levels within the BIS organizational structure when its interests are under consideration, such as the proposal for the United States to "loan" another $8.4 billion to the International Monetary Fund for funneling into communist-bloc and Third World countries. The board of directors, all superbankers themselves in their own countries, name the "president;" in the current case—Leutwiler. The board meets ten times a year and meets twice a year with communist-block countries—Poland, Yugoslavia, Hungary, Rumania, Czechoslavakia, Bulgaria, Albania and, of course, with a representative of the Soviet Union. The board's decisions not only influence but virtually control European governments—both communist and non-communist—and such international and United Nations bureaucracies as the International Monetary Fund, the Common Market and the communist-bloc Council for Mutual Economic Assistance, Comecon, the Kremlin agency for carrying out various "five year plans." For example, recently, the Kremlin, in need of hard cash currency from the West, uncharacteristically informed its Comecon partners that it was shifting its priority sales of oil from the communist-bloc to the West. It told the Comecon stooges, in effect, to grow up and start making it on their own without so much subsidy help from a hard-pressed Soviet economy. The decision left people unfamiliar with the Bank for International Settlements puzzled, wondering why Soviet Russia would be so hateful toward its little slave satellites—the reason being that the decision was not the Kremlin's but was made for the Kremlin by the board of BIS, which has no political interests but its own financial interests at heart. It intends to remain above both Moscow and Washington, to say nothing of London, Paris, Bonn and Geneva. In another instance, the Common Market, a few years ago, named a committee to study bank reserve requirements which so influence the amount of money available to a nation's economy and thus influence interest rates, prices and unemployment. The BIS board nipped it in the bud by naming its own high committee to "study" the same issue. The Common Market excused itself for stepping on "big brother's" toes and turf and abandoned the study. To this day no public report has been made of the BIS study, and none with any meaning ever will be made.

The message is clear: the world of finance and economy belongs to the BIS and no interference will be tolerated. The punishment for trespass would be financial punishment, which would mean political unpopularity for any government officials daring to trespass on the BIS. It is this kind of overwhelming and unprecedented financial power—the power to bring down men like the two of us authoring this expose or banks or even governments—that makes the Bank for International Settlements the ruler of the world. And it should be remembered that its board meets twice annually with the communist world, so to say that the communists have no influence there is to go against fact. The communists not only have strong financial influence, they have great military influence through Soviet Russia's most powerful military machine. The Bank for International Settlements, wielding such great financial force, respects other kinds of force including military (or more correctly, mostly military).

2. In addition to the powerful board of directors, the BIS has a second level of executives known as G-10 or The Group of 10, which includes not only the European bank representatives but also the Federal Reserve, the Bank of Canada and the Bank of Japan. And there is an unofficial member, somewhat like the Fed is an unofficial member of the original eight—the Saudi Arabian Monetary Authority. The G-10 grapples with the more grubby matters of interest rates, money supply, currency rates and economic growth or reduction, implementing board policy, and when it comes across a problem it can't resolve, passing it on to the higher board for decision. The G-10 then implements policy and screens out the routine so the big board won't have to bother with it.

3. Below the G-10, and taking care of its incidental requirements, is the BIS Monetary and Economic Development Department, a sort of "think tank" that answers various questions for G-10 and makes recommendations when invited to do so. It publishes a steady stream of papers and periodicals for banks throughout the world to inform them of BIS financial policy. One of its latest publications denounced the conservative free market economics championed by American economist Milton Friedman, known popularly as "supply side economics" and politically as Reaganomics. After its publication, Friedman was dropped from consideration as Federal Reserve Board chairman by the White House. Volker was invited for a visit with Reagan and subsequently was soon reappointed. Such is the power of BIS.

Before concluding that Volker and the Fed are some kind of poor relation at BIS, consider this: there is a clique of elite central bankers within the BIS who may or may not be in the structural hierarchy as just outlined but who, nevertheless, have tremendous influence and consider themselves allies of sorts in the same boat of financial interests.

At this writing, they include Volker and Henry Wallich, governor of the Fed's board of directors; Karl Pohl, president of the German Bundesbank and an official member of the BIS board; Keutwiler, of course, from both the BIS and the Swiss Bank; Lord Gordon Richardson, long-time titular head of the G-10 and former governor of the Bank of England board; Haruo Mayekawa of the Bank of Japan and Lamberto Dino of the Bank of Italy.

Rockefeller's Ruling Class

They comprise the American-Western, Europe-Japanese nucleus of David Rockefeller's independent Trilateral Commission created in 1973 to promote the economic interests of the regions represented. In fact, it is a Rockefeller effort to bring the capitalist free world further under the domination of international bankers and the Bank for International Settlements, who believe they can govern the world better without the consent of the governed.[11]

The Trilateral Commission and its counterpart, the Council on Foreign Relations—another Rockefeller funded organization promoting one-world government and one-world banking—can be seen in the context of the Bank for International Settlements not as the major non-government force in the world many of its critics contend it to be, but merely non-officio agencies, tools as it were, of the BIS of which the Rockefellers are but one of the owners and the owned.[12]

David Rockefeller once was asked if he thought there is a ruling class in the world. He answered this way:

"I really don't, I mean, there are lots of people who at any given moment in time have a major role of power in their own countries. This group is constantly changing. Certainly, if you look at the United States, I don't see that there is any ruling class. People as always, have been talking about the Eastern Establishment, whatever that may be. I suppose that I would be considered to be part of it; and yet, I'm not; I couldn't tell you what the Eastern Establishment is; and furthermore, increasingly it seems to me that the centers of influence and authority in the country are spread all over the country. I don't think that, in any real sense, there is a small group of people who are somehow gathering together and plotting what should be done for the country."[13]

Rockefeller presented too modest a picture of himself, one not shared by other international financiers who know him well. Some foreign government and financial authorities consider Rockefeller to be "a sort of invisible minister of foreign affairs" as indicated by the following interview between journalist Bill Moyers and the Saudi Arabian minister of finance in a hotel hallway outside a closed conference of Rockefeller and other international financiers at a 1980 meeting of the International

Monetary Fund members in Belgrade, Yugoslavia. The Saudi finance minister, incidentally, is one of the world's most powerful men because of his control over billions of dollars of Saudi investments throughout the world. Following is a transcript of their conversation:

MOYERS: What did you talk about with Mr. Rockefeller?

SAUDI MINISTER: Well...

MOYERS: How long have you known him?

SAUDI MINISTER: Think 14, 15 years.

MOYERS: So David Rockefeller is more than just a banker—he's a long-time friend of your country.

SAUDI MINISTER: Oh, yes.

(At this point, Rockefeller joined Moyers and the Saudi Minister in the hotel hallway).

MOYERS: Some people think that banks today are larger and more important than countries because they operate across geographical and political boundaries, and that they have become the new force in the world.

SAUDI MINISTER: Yes, yes, yes, but many of them have sort of invisible ministers of foreign affairs.

MOYERS: Invisible ministers of foreign affairs?

SAUDI MINISTER: Yes, yes, in banks, yes, you can, you cannot establish, in Chase Manhattan's case, Mr. Rockefeller, he is the Chairman and he is the...he has to do things together.[14]

In the next scene of Moyers' fascinating television profile of David Rockefeller and his "world," Moyers said, "We're not allowed to film in there (another secret meeting of International Monetary Fund members). It's a private session talking about business and, I assume, politics. Of course, we've learned this week that, in the world of David Rockefeller, it's hard to tell where business ends and politics begins."[15]

It certainly is, whether Rockefeller admits it or not. It is obvious to all financiers and government officials who deal with him and to journalists whom he allows close to him, such as Moyers, who himself is a political liberal with impeccable credentials, having been President Kennedy's press relations officer.

Rockefeller's "Morality" Exposed

One other insight into Rockefeller's "world"—he is indifferent about whether he is dealing with communists or capitalists and often has indicated that, such as during a visit to Marxist-ruled Zimbabwe when he said the politics of the country made no difference to him so long as he could do business with it. In another segment of the Moyers' profile, Rockefeller put it this way (according to the program transcript):

MOYERS: Do you ever have any qualms about dealing with an authoritarian, even repressive, government?

ROCKEFELLER: I assume that you're thinking...of moral qualms as to whether it's right for me to be dealing with people with a very different approach to life.

MOYERS: Yes, if it makes you morally uncomfortable.

ROCKEFELLER: Yes, I certainly am sometimes uncomfortable, and very uncomfortable at the things that I see; but I think that, when one becomes an international banker, one really has to cross the bridge as to whether you feel that it's the role of international banker to try to persuade other nations and people to handle their affairs in a manner that is politically or economically more to our liking. And I guess that we come to the conclusion that, even if we thought it would be desirable to do that, our chances of doing so are not very good. I personally don't see anything immoral or improper with our dealing with people with very diverse views, even if they conduct their affairs in a way that we might even find quite repugnant.[16]

Rockefeller's vast financial dealings with the slave masters in both Moscow and Peking hold no "repugnance" for him. His branch banks of Chase Manhattan in those communist capitals and his new business plaza in downtown Peking are both literally and figuratively concrete evidence of his acceptance of what he so blithely calls their "diverse views" and the way they "conduct their affairs."

Above the Law

The extensive financial trade carried on by Rockefeller and other powerful friends of communism, such as Armand Hammer of Occidental Petroleum, goes on in direct violation of the U.S. Tariff Act of 1930 that prohibits the importation into the United States of all goods and merchandise and all mined and manufactured products of any foreign country using slave labor.

The evidence that the communists are using slave labor is overwhelming, not only in the recent construction of the Soviet natural gas pipeline but also in other manufactured goods. Some half million South Vietnamese prisoners, and at least 10,000 Russian citizens who are dissidents to communist rule, now enslaved, were forced to work on the pipeline and related projects that supply Soviet industry and military installations with natural gas from Siberia and provide a supply into Western Europe that many see as a leverage for communism there.[17]

But Rockefeller, Hammer and other internationalists wield such influence in Washington that they can get away with breaking federal law. Their influence over Washington bureaucrats, especially in the State, Commerce and Treasury Departments—and, of course, with the national news media—is such that some officials think the friends of communism are right and that those who protest are "nuts."

William Van Raab, U.S. Commissioner of Customs, admitted not even knowing that the 1930 Tariff existed, much less knowing he was in part responsible for enforcing it. He did look it up, published regulations about it, and forwarded them to the Treasury Department. Going through channels, it landed before the Senior Interagency Group, of which State, Commerce and Treasury are members—the same organization that recommended that the United States could and should do nothing about the Sept. 1, 1983, South Korean Airliner massacre by the Soviet Union except make a formal diplomatic protest.

Senator William Armstrong of Colorado, whose investigations in Europe helped to reveal the story of slave labor on the pipeline, has protested U.S. foreign trade with the Soviet Union which amounted to $227.8 million in Soviet products being imported in 1982 and demanded enforcement of the 1930 Tariff Act. The stalled regulations sent by Van Raab made bureaucratic rounds, including one Treasury official who said that "only a few nuts like Armstrong" want enforcement. Armstrong immediately got forty-four other Senators, presumed "nuts" such as himself, to sign a letter to the Secretary of Treasury demanding enforcement. The Democrat party-controlled House of Representatives refused to join in the enforcement demand, so prospects for enforcement by Congressional petition is unlikely.[18]

The story illustrates the pervading influence of big international bankers such as Rockefeller and businessmen such as Hammer who deal with the communists. They are simply above the law, thanks to their influence in Washington bureaucratic and Congressional circles.

Since Watergate, it has been thought that no one was above the law, not even presidents; but it is obvious, in cases involving high-powered international finance and communism, that the likes of Rockefeller, Hammer and others who finance communism and profit from it are far beyond the laws of any one nation.

When it is considered that Rockefeller is only a cog in the big wheel of world financial domination by the Bank for International Settlements, the power of that most powerful bank is obvious. It controls Rockefeller and his Trilateral Commission and Council for Foreign Relations. It controls the Federal Reserve, whose chairman pays tribute monthly at the bank in Switzerland. It controls the Treasury, Commerce, and State Department bureaucracies, as shown by their flippant attitudes toward law enforcement when big money and communism are involved.

The media dares not call this unique set of circumstances and events a "*conspiracy*." There is little, if any, explanation offered for it by the media. Criticism of it, and even senatorial demands for enforcement and reform, are brushed off as the raving of "nuts," and *that* is publicized by the media to perpetuate such propaganda about those who oppose the perversion of freedom by either communism or international finance or both.

The Money Shrine
The shrine of world financial control is a new eighteen-story

32

headquarters in Basel which houses the Bank for International Settlements. It has a sub-basement fallout shelter to protect and preserve the world's central bankers so they can rule the post-nuclear holocaust world just as they rule now. The headquarters with its twenty miles of tunnel vaults is self-contained and fully air-conditioned, the shelter is stocked with food and water and communications supplies, and the entire facility is equipped with a triple fire extinguishing system so no outside firemen are necessary. It has its own hospital and staff.

There is a restaurant on the top floor with a view of three countries—Germany, France and Switzerland. It is private and is used only when the bank's directors and G-10 and the Monetary and Economic Development Department officials and staff are in session ten times yearly.

Other floors on this most exclusive of buildings are occupied by plush executive suites equipped for both living accommodations and offices, each complete with computers and staffs and international communications. Meeting rooms, computer rooms, staff offices and other business administration necessities occupy the remainder of the building.

This is a far cry from the old headquarters in downtown Basel that the BIS occupied until 1977. In the old days, business was conducted in a non-descript, five-story building—the business offices on the top four floors and a chocolate shop open to the public occupying the ground floor. But one couldn't get from the chocolate shop to upstairs. Entrance was through a building next door that used to be a public hotel but was taken over by the bank to accommodate the central bankers and staffs when they assembled. Access to the bank offices was from adjoining above-ground floors of the ex-hotel. These humble and unmarked accommodations, except for the chocolate shop sign, helped to maintain the privacy and secrecy of the world's most powerful bank until need for additional space necessitated construction of the new headquarters and resultant publicity.[19]

The Secret Realm

The outsider who probably knows more about the bank than anyone else is investigative journalist and author Edward Jay Epstein, who wrote *Legend*, a book exposing the communist training and secret code name of Lee Harvey Oswald, alleged assassin of President Kennedy, and *News From Nowhere*, exposing news media manipulation and propaganda use of national and world events. Explaining why the Bank for International Settlements is useful to the world's international bankers who control their nations' money and economies, Epstein says:

"One answer is, of course, secrecy. By co-mingling part of their reserves in what amounts to a gigantic mutual fund of short-term investments, the central banks create a convenient screen behind which they can hide their own deposits and withdrawals in financial centers around the world. For example, if the BIS places funds in Hungary, the individual national central banks do not have to answer to their governments for investing in a communist country. And the central banks are apparently willing to pay a high fee to use the cloak of the BIS.''[20]

That "high fee" is more than just money if the organization of the BIS is any indication. It most likely includes surrender of major financial and economic decisions to the board of directors of BIS and its G-10 and economic-monetary support. Because of the banks' secrecy, having to answer to no one—not to stockholders, the public, the media, or any government or regulatory agency—it is not known, and may never be known, whether the national central banks such as Federal Reserve own the BIS or the BIS owns them. It is most probable that they are all one and the same.

Knowing this, and we can safely presume it is a most valid assumption, until the BIS elects to make public its most secret records, we are in a position to more readily understand the world currency system, as established at Bretton Woods and later revised at the Smithsonian Institution meeting, and the current free-floating policy; the United Nations and its International Monetary Fund; the powerful private bank known as the Federal Reserve which controls American banking and currency; and the BIS's relationship with such as the Rockefellers and the private kingdoms of the Trilateral Commission and the Council on Foreign Relations.

In such a powerful and secret realm, anything is possible. Money is power and begets corruption. From the money center of the world at the Bank for International Settlements, tentacles reach out to control the news and news media, culture and entertainment, academics and education, politics and government—all the things that go into shaping and molding public opinion. It makes doing business with communism seem acceptable. It makes communism seem acceptable. It could make a cosmetic merger of communism and capitalism see acceptable.

If money is at the root of all evil, then the Bank for International Settlements and its secret meetings and subterranean vaults for riches and nuclear shelter of those who control them could be the taproot. We will know when this biggest and most secret bank in all the world opens itself to public scrutiny. Meanwhile, read on, but don't hold your breath until the big bank goes public.

Chapter 2

THE FEDERAL RESERVE: CRADLE OF COMMUNISM AND OTHER CONSPIRACIES

The Red Double Cross

It seems incredible but the Federal Reserve System, established to control American currency and economy, may well have been the cradle of the communist revolution in Russia and has continued to be its best friend and supporter.

The privately-owned Federal Reserve is the central bank for American banking, just as the privately-owned Bank of England has been the central bank for the British Empire throughout its many ups and downs.

The United States government has no control over the operation of the Federal Reserve. In fact, the reverse is more likely since the Federal Reserve controls the money. It's the old, old story dating back to medieval times and beyond—the king (the government) spends more money than he has, so he must put the government in debt to the people who have money to lend, namely, international bankers, who over the centuries have built up huge fortunes loaning money to various governments, usually to pay for wars.

This was the same manner in which the birth of the communist revolution in Russia was financed, by international bankers seeking to make a profit without regard to political or patriotic allegiance.

Here is what happened:

During World War I, the poorly-equipped and even more poorly-led army of Russia's ruler, Czar Nicholas II, was beaten on the Eastern Front with losses running into the millions of men and was on the verge of mutiny. It was this opportunity to seize power from a failing government and army that Lenin, Trotsky, and their Bolshevik followers, who had been plotting against the Czar for years, used to their advantage.

But they desperately needed money and double crossed both the Allies and Germany to get it. The Germans reasoned that, if the Bolsheviks

35

succeeded in overthrowing the Czar, Russia would quit the war and relieve the pressure on the Eastern Front; the Allies reasoned that, if the weak Czarist government was replaced by a stronger revolutionary government, Russia could be bolstered financially and politically to stay in the war against Germany.

Lenin and his then fellow-revolutionary sidekick Trotsky played both sides, accepting money from both Germany and the Allies to finance their revolution against the Czar. They never had any intention of carrying on a war against Germany once they toppled the Czar, but the Allies were not certain of that even if they many have suspected it.

The German funds for the Russian revolutionaries came from the Hamburg banking house of M. M. Warburg. The Allied funds came from the international financial and banking interests of the Rothschilds, doing business during the war through the Federal Reserve and the Bank of England, both of which they dominated and still do.

Banks Need War

It is ironic that, while the German bank of Warburg was delivering money to the revolutionaries in Sweden and Switzerland, a member of the Warburg family, Paul Warburg, the first chairman of the Federal Reserve Board in the United States, was arranging for the delivery of money to the revolutionaries' agents in New York. Paul Warburg's brother was head of the German Secret Service. He is the official who made it possible for Lenin to leave Switzerland in a secret, closed train, cross wartime Germany unmolested, and enter Russia (train and all) to lead the revolution and kill the Czar and his family, looting the Russian treasury as a spoil to the victors.

As fiscal agent for the United States government (the American taxpayers), the private Federal Reserve Bank prospered in its early growth years due to the war. That's what central banks are all about—financing war.

For centuries, the central banks of Europe financed war after war to their profit. The House of Rothschild was the biggest winner of the Napoleonic wars that ravaged Europe for years, making unconscionable profits on loans to England, Prussia, Austria and Russia in their alliance to defeat Napoleon and the French Revolution which threatened crowned heads throughout the continent.[2]

Who Owns The Fed?

Who owns the Federal Reserve System of banking, currency and economic control in the United States? For years it was one of the world's best-kept secrets. Most Americans still don't know. If they think about it at all, they assume, mistakenly, that the government owns it. The fact that the U.S. economy is owned by international bankers with no political or patriotic allegiance to America is incomprehensible to many

Americans. But that's the truth, and that truth explains much about the trouble this country is in—a $1 trillion plus national debt expected to total more than $3 trillion by the year 2000; multi-billion dollar federal deficits each year that obviously are beyond the control of presidents and Congress; a continual flow of foreign aid or transfer of wealth from the United States to communist and Third World countries, partly through the drain of the United Nations' International Monetary Fund and World Bank; the loss of such major industries as steel and automobile manufacturing and textiles to overseas interests; and the buildup of Soviet military power beyond the strength of U.S. defense.

Who owns the Federal Reserve? Here is the answer:

• The Rothschild Bank of London and Berlin, whose American agents since Civil War times included the J. P. Morgan banking interests and their current financial descendants such as Morgan Guaranty Trust and the Drexel bankers of Philadelphia.

• Kuhn, Loeb Co., a leading international financier out of New York by way of Cincinnati. Kuhn, Loeb, with the backing of the Rothschilds, financed most railroad construction and consolidation in America during the 19th Century when railroads were the nation's biggest business.

• Lazard Freres of Paris, another Rothschild spinoff.

• Warburg Bank of Hamburg, Germany, and Amsterdam, The Netherlands.

• Lehman Brothers Bank of New York, a firm that came to prominence during World War I financing, reaping tremendous profits then and since. Herbert Lehman of the firm, later U.S. Senator from New York, was on the General Staff of the U.S. Army in World War I, although without previous military experience. He was an early student and admirer of communism, advocating adoption of much of its centralized control planning for the American economy.

• Israel Moses Seif Banks of Italy, another wartime financier.

• Goldman, Sachs Bank of New York.

• Chase Manhattan Bank of New York, a Rockefeller bank.

•There are about 300 people, all quite well-known to one another, who hold private stock or shares in the Federal Reserve Bank system. They comprise the American branch of the interlocking, international banking cartel operated out of the Bank for International Settlements in Switzerland. These are the money rulers who finance both capitalism and communism for profit without scruples about politics or patriotism.[3]

Unbelievable? A series of congressional court decisions establishing case law says this is true:

1. The fact that the Federal Reserve Board regulates the Reserve Banks does not make it a federal agency.[4]

2. The government shall in no way attempt to carry on through its own mechanism the routine operations and banking which require detailed knowledge of local and individual credit and which determines the funds of a community in any given instance. In other words, the reserve bank plan retains to the government power over the exercise of the broader bank functions, while it leaves to individuals and privately-owned institutions the actual direction of routine.[5]

3. Each Federal Reserve Bank is a separate corporation owned by commercial banks.[6]

4. Federal Reserve Bank activities include collecting and clearing checks, making advances to private and commercial entities, holding reserves for member banks, discounting the notes of member banks, and buying and selling securites on the open market.[7]

The Federal Reserve Bank makes no bones about its control of the currency system or money in America. In its own publications it makes its control quite clear:

"Who creates money? Changes in the quantity of money may originate with actions of the Federal Reserve System (the central bank), depository institutions (principally the commercial banks), or the public, but the major control rests with the central bank."[8]

Power Is The Key

The ownership of the Federal Reserve is actually not as important financially as the control of Federal Reserve policy that ownership bestows. The Federal Reserve "stock" owned by the bankers is more like a tax or a levy that the bankers pay to the Fed and, in return, receive a mere six percent dividend. The "stock", in effect, is like a subscription to inside information about the monetary policy being set by the Federal Reserve's board of governors. This advance information on Fed policy allows the banker-owners of the Fed to make a killing in speculation, with advance information from the Fed.

The late Congressman Wright Patman, a long-time foe of the Fed, once explained the difference between Federal Reserve stock and ordinary stock as perceived by shareholders. He said:

"First, it carries no proprietary interests. In this respect, the stock is unlike the stock of any private corporation.

Second, it cannot be sold or pledged for loans. It thus does not represent an ownership claim.

Third, in the event of the dissolution of the Federal Reserve banks, as provided for in the Federal Reserve Act, the net assets, after payment of the stock, go to the U.S. Treasury rather than the private banks.

Fourth, the stock does not carry the ordinary voting rights of stock. The method of electing the officers of the Federal Reserve banks is, in no way, connected to the amount of stock ownership. Instead, each bank in a district has one vote within its classification, regardless of its stock ownership."[9]

The ownership of the Fed, as such, is not the important thing financially. It is the control of the nation's money and credit and economy, along with access to advance information about what the control policy is going to be, that makes Federal Reserve ownership so valuable to the owners of the Federal Reserve and their master bank, the Bank for International Settlements.

The Money Engineers

With control of American money well-established by the Federal Reserve Act of 1913, the year before World War I broke out in Europe, the Fed was in a position by 1917, the year of the Russian Revolution, to act as a conduit of funds to Lenin, Trotsky and the Bolsheviks. Using the Rothschild method of transferring huge amounts of money by paper writ instead of actually moving the cash itself, the Fed extended virtually unlimited credit to the communists—the same kind of "Special Drawing Right" used today by "customers," that is, freeloading beneficiaries of the U.N.'s International Monetary Fund.

This amazing Federal Reserve financing of communism was directed by Paul Warburg, who had resigned as Fed board chairman during World War I due to his German background and the fact his brother headed the German Secret Service. Warburg returned to a $500,000-a-year job with Kuhn, Loeb Co. and was appointed by President Woodrow Wilson to head the Federal Advisory Council (which through its recommendations directed Federal Reserve Policy) and chairman of the executive committee of the American Acceptance Council. ("Acceptances" was the term used to describe international transfers of funds by commercial paper instead of bond-secured currency, made possible only by establishment of a central bank, the Fed).

Engineering the financing of communist Russia under Warburg's direction was Henry L. Stimson, Warburg's lawyer who set up for him control of an acceptance trust, as well as a chemical trust. Stimson would go on to high public office in the future, including Secretary of State for President Herbert Hoover and Secretary of War for President Franklin Roosevelt, effortlessly crossing political party lines.

It was Stimson and his law partner Bronson Winthrop who served as liaison between American financial interests represented by the Federal Reserve and their refinancing of Russia, torn by war and revolution. In the 1920s, Stimson and Winthrop made the communist currency, called *rubles*, respectable on foreign currency exchanges with their banker-backed blank checks on the Federal Reserve. It was Stimson (who also had served as Secretary of State to President Taft, 1908-1912) who carried on informal diplomatic relations for the bankers with the communist rulers of Russia during the 1920s and had paved the way for formal government diplomatic recognition of the Soviets by President Roosevelt when he took office in 1933.[10]

Kremlin "Trusts" Established

Once diplomatic recognition had been achieved, the unlimited financing of communist Russia could be carried on through official channels. The tax money of the American working public has poured into the Soviet Union to finance communism to the tune of more than $80 billion since then, much of it in supposed "lend-lease" during World War II that has never been, and never will be, repaid. More of it went to the Soviets in the form of Fort Knox gold during the London "Gold Pool" manipulation of the 1960s, when America's bullion store disappeared.[11]

Warburg's trusts were based on central control. The largest was the International Acceptance Bank for administering international finance, including establishment of communist "trusts" or nationalization of industry and business in Russia by the Bolsheviks. They were the appropriate types of administrative vehicles the communists found necessary in order to conduct the business of government and the communist economy. A London magazine revealed this startling "trust" concept in a story in 1922 which said, in part:

"During the past year, practically every single capitalistic institution in Russia has been restored. This is true of the State Bank, private banking, the Stock Exchange, the right to possess money, the right of inheritance, the bill of exchange system, and other institutions and practices involved in the conduct of private industry and trade. A great part of the former nationalized industries are now found in semi-independent trusts."[12]

This story is one of the few publicized indications of international financial control over the Russian Revolution. The world bankers not only financed Lenin and Trotsky, through Warburg and Stimson and Winthrop, they established a trust management of the Russian economy that made it possible and acceptable to send vast amounts of money and technical help from the United States to communist Russia in its infancy.

This was indeed something new in the world, not just another revolution (revolutions were becoming old hat), but a historical opportunity to establish a centrally-controlled state from its inception, without an intervening period of some other form of government!

This is what the communists and their liberal friends were talking about when they came back from their visits to Russia in the 1920s and 1930s saying, "I have seen the future and it works."

It was this central control, with no interference by public opinion, with no demands for democratic representation, that appealed to the socialist-minded planners of a worldly utopia. Here was their chance, through communist style and trust organization financed by the money controllers of the world, to establish the perfect society. Of course, the planners would call the shots, or the bankers would, or the communists would; but, at least, the people with their diverse ideas would not.

This was the communist babe, with its trust economy, that sucked the milk of the Federal Reserve and other central banks of the world and still does today, even though it has grown into a hulking adult. It is this unnatural creature of Satan that went on a world-wide rampage, killing 142 million people in the process, like some giant Godzilla stomping through a miniature movie set.

FDR's German Role

It is little wonder that Franklin D. Roosevelt extended diplomatic recognition to Soviet Russia when he was elected president of the United States, for he was one of the international bankers who had speculated in German war reparations payments after World War I and floated massive foreign bonds in the United States for international finance reconstruction, including the beginning of modernization in the Soviet Union. The Czar had been of the old world and considered too inefficient to administer modernization, so the international financiers who would invest in Russia had put the communist-trust management in place through the revolution.

The 1920s editions of the New York Director of Directors lists Franklin D. Roosevelt as president and director of United European Investors Ltd. in 1923 and 1924, a firm that floated millions of dollars of German war reparations bonds in the United States, all of which were virtually useless, to begin with, because of Germany's post-war economy; and all of which were defaulted by Hitler's Third Reich. Poor's Directory of Directors, a forerunner of Standard and Poor, lists Roosevelt as a director of the International Germanic Trust Co. in 1928, still dabbling in the war reparations business.

Roosevelt's law partner, during the 1920s, was Basil O'Connor who was a director of Cuban-American Manganese Corp., Honduras Timber Corp., West Indies Sugar Corp., Federal International Corp. (almost as official sounding a name as Federal Reserve), Warm Springs Foundation and the American Red Cross, which collects millions of dollars of donations annually from the American people. Roosevelt's establishment of a "Good Neighbor Policy" for Latin America can be seen in light of his partner's financial interests as something more than just pure good will.

And, incidentally, when Roosevelt took office as president, he appointed Stimson as Secretary of War; and as director of the federal budget, he named James Paul Warburg, son of the Paul Warburg who essentially wrote the Federal Reserve Act. There apparently was no concern at the time that the U.S. budget director also was vice-president of his father's International Acceptance Corp., perhaps the world's biggest commercial banking paper trust that was deeply involved, by then, with the new Bank for International Settlements.[13]

The Federal Reserve nurtured world communism. It helped to finance the revolution. It had a hand in establishing the communist-trust operation of the Soviet economy. It played a role in U.S. diplomatic recognition of Soviet Russia.

The Sordid Story

The Federal Reserve is the culmination of a 125-year-old fight to establish a central bank in the United States. Americans, having escaped control of central banks in Europe which fostered wars and enriched themselves on the waste and bloodshed, traditionally had opposed creation of a central bank. The purpose of a central bank is basically to mobilize a nation's currency and economy for war by central or virtually dictatorial control. This is what the people of America did not want. This is the story of how they got it anyway:

If there is one characteristic of a central bank such as the Federal Reserve, it is its necessary dependence upon war. Alexander Hamilton persuaded a reluctant George Washington to approve this country's pioneer central bank, the First Bank of the United States, as an instrument for financing post-Revolutionary War reconstruction. It may have seemed like a good idea at the time, but the private and secret ownership of the bank led to abuse and corruption. When Thomas Jefferson became president, he broke it like the rotten egg it was.

The Second Bank of the United States was conceived by Nicholas Biddle with the support of James Rothschild of Paris as an instrument for financing post-War of 1812 reconstruction. The money control and abuse of this bank led to President Andrew Jackson's long fight to close it, during which a government Sub-Treasury System was established, ostensibly, to keep government funds out of the hands of bankers and their international partners.

During the American Civil War, President Abraham Lincoln, rather than turn to bankers demanding up to twenty-eight percent interest for funds to finance the war, issued federal "Greenbacks," paper money eventually authorized by the National Bank Act of 1864, pledging the "Greenbacks" would be paid for with gold once the war was over. At one time, when the Union's war fortunes were at low ebb, the paper Confederate money was worth more on international money exchanges than Lincoln's "Greenbacks;" but with eventual Union victory, the Confederate money became worthless; and the government began the long and, at times, almost impossible task of making the "Greenbacks" as good as gold.

Manipulating Panic

To prevent that from happening during the post-Civil War period, the proponents of a central bank, with the collusion of their international banking partners, shipped vast amounts of gold outside the United States periodically in an effort to destroy the "Greenbacks" and the currency and economy of the nation in order to create a demand for monetary reform and a central bank to administer it. It was these manipulations, primarily, that caused the financial panics of 1873, 1893 and, finally, 1907. A profitable by-product for the gold and money manipulators was the decline in prices of various securities. The manipulators would purchase these securities at bargain prices and sell them when their value had risen again after the panics were over.[4]

Speculation in economics is one thing, but manipulation is something else altogether, implying a form of financial control. The so-called "money trust" of the 19th century, headed by Morgan and Rockefeller—both financed by Rothschild and the international banking cartel centered in Europe—were pikers compared with the now centralized and consolidated power of the owners of the Federal Reserve and the Bank for International Settlements.

Concealment for Corruption

No amount of regulation can overcome greed and sin in this world. Every economic "boom" is followed by a "bust" no matter how fancy the words may be, used to camouflage the tragedy. The Federal Reserve and its misnamed "open market committee" operate in complete secrecy. News reporters are not allowed to attend. The public is banned. This kind of concealment assures an environment for insider dealing, abuse and corruption.

It's the same old story. New opportunities for profits are seized upon and greed causes them to be over-exploited. A manic boom results and too many people try to get in on it too late with too much money at stake. The financial system becomes overloaded in whatever area is booming—gold, silver, real estate, stocks, certain commodities—and prices start to fall, causing a rush or panic to get out before the collapse.

During the mania, people (or banks or other financial interests) with wealth or access to big credit, and acting as stewards of others' money, turn that money into whatever asset is booming. Then, in the panic, they change back to money or debt repayment; and the crash occurs, disastrously driving down the price of whatever had been the subject of the boom. It's the uninformed public, the average investor, who gets hurt because he had no inside information and acted too late. Often life savings disappear. The investor with inside information from confidential decision-making and control sources knows about the latest manipulations and can get in and then out at the most profitable times.[15]

Financial Flops

Two fairly recent financial debacles that come to mind, as a result of greed and poor stewardship, are the collapse of Penn Central Bank in Oklahoma City due to over-investment in oil speculation, and the ruination of Drysdale Securities, which cost Rockefeller's Chase

Manhattan Bank depositors millions because of lost gambles in financial securities.

Chase lost one quarter of a billion dollars in the Drysdale debacle because Rockefeller junior executives didn't know that, as agents for Drysdale, they assumed responsibility for Drysdale's wheeling and dealing that lost the most money on the least capital in the shortest time in the history of Wall Street. With a capital of only $20 million, Drysdale lost about $4 billion in three months with Chase's "help."[16]

This is the same Rockefeller who lobbied so long and hard and successfully for the appointment of the last half dozen chairmen of the wheeling and dealing Federal Reserve!

A major reason why so many Americans are uninformed about the Federal Reserve, to say nothing of the Bank for International Settlements and their secret and private methods of conducting business and manipulating money, is that the public schools and the textbooks they have used have failed to accurately teach the facts about them.

Education Failures

A major American history textbook used by thousands of school systems and studied by millions of pupils during the late 1920s and well into the late 1940s and early 1950s was *The Growth of A Nation*. It has fewer than 100 words about the Federal Reserve in a book of more than 700 pages, and even those words are so bland and uncritical that they are almost totally misleading.[17]

After World War II, a new American history textbook entered the field and was studied by millions more American pupils—Charles and Mary Beard's *History of the United States, A Study in American Civilization*. Despite having had the benefit of another decade or so experience with the Fed, the Beards' book of 700-plus pages included fewer than 200 words about it and was equally dry and misleading without any critical analysis.[18]

In retrospect, it seems almost tragically comic that the 1934 edition of *The Growth of A Nation* (first published in 1928, the year before the stock market crash and subsequent Great Depression) had this to say in the midst of the depression when it was published:

"The Federal Reserve Board studies banking and currency with the aim of protecting the country from financial panics."[19]

Small wonder that with such inadequate teaching and textbooks on such an important subject as the American currency and economy, millions of Americans mistakenly believe the Federal Reserve—if they ever think of it at all— is some kind of government agency when it is in fact a privately-owned bank unconstitutionally sanctioned by Congress to do its currency work for it.

The Fradulent Fed

We say "unconstitutionally" because the Federal Reserve Act approved by Congress in 1913, authorizing private bankers to take over the currency issuance and control of U.S. money, was and is in violation of Article I Section 8 of the Constitution which says, "The Congress shall have power to coin money, regulate the value thereof, and of foreign coin, and fix the standard of weights and measures."

Congress abdicated that responsibility in 1913 and has never moved to regain it.

The Board of Governors of the Federal Reserve promotes the deception that it is some kind of federal agency but at times reveals itself for what it truly is—a private and independent *trustee* (and that word is debatable) of the nation's credit and monetary affairs.

Following is an excerpt from one of the board's publications, and we have inserted our comment after each sentence:

"The framers of the Federal Reserve Act, passed in 1913, took precautions to see that monetary policy would be, insofar as possible, impartial, informed and in the interest of the country as a whole."

COMMENT: The Federal Reserve Bank and System can hardly be considered "impartial" because it is a banker's bank, created by and for bankers, completely independent from public scrutiny or control. Ask your congressman if he or any of his colleagues, or for that matter the President or any other government official, has any control over the Federal Reserve. His honest answer can only be "no."

"The Congress took care to safeguard money management from becoming a device that could be controlled by private interests, on the one hand, or by partisan political interests, on the other."

COMMENT: What a laugh! The Federal Reserve is owned and controlled by private interests. Partisan political interests are immaterial because the bankers who own the Fed will do as they see fit in their own interests without any consideration of political or patriotic consequences. They are indeed beyond any kind of political control.

"For example, the fourteen-year terms of the Boards of governors help to insulate decisions from day-to-day political pressures."

COMMENT: We might add the board also is quite well-insulated from the public whose money it controls. And doesn't a fourteen-year term seem excessive? That's two years longer than three presidential terms, eight years longer than a senatorial term and twelve years longer than a term in the House of Representatives.

"Broadly, the Reserve System may be likened to a trusteeship created by the Congress to make policy for, and to administer and regulate, the nation's credit and monetary affairs."[20]

COMMENT: This is the most honest sentence of the statement. A trustee is someone to whom another's property or the management of another's property is entrusted. Unfortunately, this "trust" that Congress put in the Federal Reserve to "safeguard money management" in "the interest of the country as a whole" has been in large part responsible for the nation's involvement in the worst wars in its history and the worst economic depressions and recessions it has ever known. Some management! Some trustee!

The Federal Reserve System is governed by a seven-member board located in Washington and twelve Federal Reserve regional banks and their twenty-five branches. The system employs about 25,000 people and has an operating budget of $700 million. Its responsibility under the act creating it is the conduct of monetary policy, meaning action to influence the economy by affecting the cost, supply and availability of money and credit. We will explain how that is done in the following chapter about money. The Fed supervises and loosely regulates commercial banking and a form of payments mechanism it contends is responsive to the nation's domestic and international financial needs and objectives.[21]

The Treacherous Tools

The two major tools used to exercise the Fed's power are reserve requirements and discount rates. The Fed's board alone decides the reserve requirement—that is, the percentage of deposits—which banks and other depository institutions must hold in their vaults to meet any demands for the deposits. If this percentage is set high, say twenty per cent or so, money and credit are tight; but a low percentage makes for easy money, or as some economists say, inflationary money. This is the way the amount of money in circulation can be controlled. The discount rate—the interest rate at which depositor institutions can borrow money from the Reserve Banks—can be set by boards of the individual Federal Reserve regional banks and branches, subject to approval by the board of governors.[22]

In plainer language, what Americans should understand about this private control of money is that the reserve requirements can determine whether the economy booms or busts, depending upon the interest of the bankers who make the decision; and the discount rate or interest rate is nothing more than the private Federal Reserve bankers charging citizens for use of their own money. It means the banks and bankers of the Federal Reserve get an interest slice off every dollar you use.

But worst and most amazing and unbelievable of all is the way the Federal Reserve makes money out of nothing! Makes it out of thin air! In effect, does it with mirrors! We will show how that is done in the next chapter on money.

How this incredible state of affairs came about is a matter of record and history, even if it's not in the conventional history and economics textbooks. After all, when you expose the truth about the greatest financial swindle in history, and the swindler happens to be the interest that controls

46

the money upon which you are dependent, you are obviously treading upon thin ice. Today's modern, urbane and sophisticated Federal Reserve Board of Governors would as soon the public not know about the Fed's shady past and its inception based on the greed and self-interest of the board's banking predecessors. Banks don't care much for anything that reflects on banking integrity, but we are convinced it is incumbent upon us to inform our readers of the powerful and ruthless, criminal and conspiratorial hoax that brought about creation of the unconstitutional Federal Reserve.

The Cynical Creation

Creation of the Federal Reserve System was largely J.P. Morgan's, which is to say Rothschild's, doing. Nothing important in American banking happened in the late 19th and early 20th centuries without Morgan's knowledge and approval. Following the panic of 1907, Congress authorized a National Monetary Commission to draw up a plan for reform of the American money and banking system. The chairman was Senator Nelson Aldrich of Rhode Island, a partner in the Duke tobacco trust and the Rockefeller-Guggenheim rubber trust, both indebted to Morgan. (Incidentally, the late U.S. Vice-President Nelson Aldrich Rockefeller was named in honor of Senator Aldrich, his maternal grandfather, whose daughter married into the Rockefeller family.) The commission spent two years in Europe at taxpayer expense studying European centralized banking. When the commission returned from Europe in 1910, it didn't report to Congress, its creator, but instead Aldrich and certain commission staff members met secretly with Morgan at Jekyll Island, Georgia, to draft the new banking and monetary plan under Morgan's direction.[23]

The first plan, drafted by Aldrich and named *Suggested Plan for Monetary Legislation*, was rejected by the Congress that met in 1911 and 1912 because it did not provide for Congressional oversight; and the Democrats, confident they would gain control of the White House in 1912, wanted to delay any reform until they were in national power to direct it (or so they thought).[24]

Morgan then turned the final drafting over to Paul Warburg, a partner in Kuhn, Loeb Co. which at the time controlled through finance the major American railroads, the nation's largest business. As early as 1910, Warburg had written a plan for what he called the "United Reserve Bank of the United States" and had published it in the New York Times nine months before the conspirators met at Jekyll Island. It called for worldwide control of finances, world branch banks, a governing board to set reserve requirements and interest rates and to make currency policy. With various modifications to make the plan more palatable to the Congress and the public, it was Warburg's plan that eventually was adopted by Congress and became the Federal Reserve Act. [25]

Other conspirators at Jekyll Island who helped shape and draft the plan included the following:

BENJAMIN STRONG, president of the Morgan-controlled Bankers Trust of New York, who was to become the first governor of the New York Federal Resident Bank, keystone of the system. Strong had been financialy instrumental in consolidation of Rothschild's interests in the United States in 1901 under the name of Northern Securities Trust, a deception intended to hide the Rothschild-Morgan control of railroads.

CHARLES D. NORTON, president of Morgan's First National Bank of New York.

FRANK VANDERLIP, president of National City Bank of New York, owned by Kuhn, Loeb and Rockefeller oil interests. He headed the Cuban sugar trust after the Spanish-American War.

A. PLATT ANDREW, an economist on the staff of the National Monetary Commission.

HENRY P. DAVISON, a senior partner in J.P. Morgan and Co.

These were the major conspirators who drafted the Federal Reserve Act in their interest and submitted it to Congress in the name of the National Monetary Commission. It was not the congressional commission's report but Morgan's and Rothschild's and Warburg's and, only incidentally, Aldrich's. Congress was little more than a rubber stamp for the act which took on the name of Carter Glass and Robert Owen, chairmen, respectively, of the the Senate and House Banking and Finance Committees, although they had nothing to do with it except pushing it through their committees and Congress. [26]

Col. Ely Garrison, long-time London agent of Brown Brothers, New York bankers, and an adviser to President Wilson who had signed the Federal Reserve Act into law, later wrote in an article entitled "The Federal Reserve Law" saying:

"Paul Warburg is the man who got the Federal Reserve Act together after the Aldrich Plan aroused so much national resentment and opposition. The mastermind of both plans was Baron Alfred Rothschild of London."[27]

Warburg's son James Paul Warburg, who was federal budget director in FDR's administration and also a top campaign adviser for Eisenhower, has written many books loaded with communist and socialist propaganda. He became a leader of the United World Federalists (a one-world government movement) and often has said in his writings and in newspaper interviews:

"It is not a question of IF we will have one-world government, it is only a question of WHEN."

As if the legacy of the Federal Reserve founders represented by the likes of Warburg, the younger, was not enough; we have, at this writing, Paul Volcker as chairman of the Federal Reserve. Volcker represents big banking interests, having been a Chase Manhattan (Rockefeller) bank executive before serving as Under Secretary of the Treasury to Presidents Kennedy, Johnson, Nixon and Ford, then was appointed Fed chairman by Carter and reappointed by Reagan. He has served both Democrats and Republicans and in 1983 beat out several notable conservative economists for the job when Reagan reappointed him as Fed chairman. It seems obvious that partisan politics has little to do with his job, but money does.

Volcker had succeeded G. William Miller, a Rockefeller friend, who had succeeded Arthur Burns, formerly Arthur Burnsieg, an Austrian economist who changed his name and became influential in the Rockefeller-controlled Council on Foreign Relations. Burns had succeeded William Chesney Martin, another member of Rockefeller's Council on Foreign Relations. The control of the Federal Reserve by big bankers stretches back in history to its founding. [28]

Fooling the Public

Another thing the Federal Reserve chairmen have in common, besides being the tools of big banking interests, is the ability to double-talk in order to fool the press and the public into thinking the Fed's worthless paper money is actually worth something. Here are some examples:

Volcker, Nov. 13, 1979: "We are now placing more emphasis on controlling the provision of reserves to the banking system...to keep monetary growth within our established targets." The "target" for fourth-quarter to fourth-quarter growth in 1979-80 was 6.5 percent but the actual growth was 7.2 percent; 1980-81 target, 6 to 8.5 percent, actual 5.1 percent; 1981-82 target, 2.5 to 5.5 percent, actual 8.5 percent. Over those fiscal years Volcker was never once within his predicted "target"; which is to say he either doesn't know what he is doing or else deliberately misleads the public with his predictions so Fed owners and their insider friends can make financial killings while the mass of public investors go the other way under Volcker's phony predictions.

Miller, July 28, 1978: "Monetary policy has been designed to restrain inflation. But monetary policy alone cannot do the job." And Miller again on Nov. 16, 1978: "You can be assured that monetary policy will do its part in achieving that objective." The facts were that, during Miller's term of office from March 1978 to August 1979, the money supply grew by 8.6 percent and inflation rose 11.1 percent—the exact opposites of what he said the Fed was planning to do.

Burns, Feb. 19, 1971: "While a high rate of growth of the narrowly-defined money supply may well be appropriate for brief periods, rates of increase above the 5 to 6 percent range—if continued for a long period of time—have typically intensified inflationary presssures. The Federal Reserve will not become the architects of a new wave of inflation." The facts reveal that, during the next two years, the money supply grew 8.1 percent, during the next seven years, 6.4 percent, while inflation increased during the next two years (under price controls) 3.5 percent and during the next seven years by 6.8 percent.

Martin, Feb. 26, 1969: "I am optimistic about the prospects for gradual success of the stabilization policies now in force." The facts show that, during the two years before that statement, inflation had increased by 4.0 percent; but, during the next two years, it rose 5.7 percent. [29]

These Federal Reserve Chairmen, dating back some 15 years, are either total incompetents or deliberate liars or maybe both. None of them have ever told the public the whole truth about the Fed's monetary policies and, in fact, have misled and misdirected anyone listening to them in every case!

The reason for these lies becomes clear in the light of monetary history during the past 15 years: the Federal Reserve has deliberately destroyed the dollar once based on gold and substituted for it a dollar based on paper. [30]

The lies or inaccuracies or miscalculations or sheer blunders by the Federal Reserve's top officials over the years finally prompted the Fed itself under Volcker to devise yet another scheme to mislead the public, the White House, the Treasury Department and the Congress.

The "Monitoring" Malarkey

After December, 1982, when financial institutions were for the first time allowed to offer money market deposit accounts, and January 1983, when they also got authority for Super NOW (negotiable order of withdrawal) accounts, the Fed abandoned for the moment the old terminology of "target" to set the range of the money supply and subsequent inflation and introduced the word "monitoring." This kind of word trickery would give the Fed broader discretion and an even more vague area within which to place its "predictions."

Under the new "monitoring" guise, the Fed claimed it could not be certain just what the impact of the new type of accounts would have on the money supply of the nation. The Fed told America that the money supply would remain about the same as the new accounts would offset one another in the Fed's money supply descriptions or classifications known as M1, M2 and M3 (which in themselves show the Fed can't define money). The Fed was once again wrong, as usual, as M1, the main money supply, shot sky high, blowing Fed predictions and "monitoring" all to pieces. The Fed is always wrong, perhaps deliberately wrong, so as to mislead the public. This allows the Fed's friends with access to its secret deliberations to make investments that capitalize upon inside information while the public is given misinformation.

Economists, who like to live in the make-believe world that paper money is real money and has some relation to the economy, furrowed their brows and wrung their collective hands along with the financial writers of the *Washington Post*, the mouthpiece of the Federal Reserve, as they pretended not to know what had happened.

"No one has an answer that can be conclusive," the *Washington Post* reported.[31]

The *Post*, and later the Fed, following the *Post's* suggestion, concluded that the new accounts made deposits in M1 seem more attractive than first believed and that a large amount of money formerly in M2 deposits were transferred into M1.[32]

What marlarkey! There was no massive transfer of deposits or funds from M1 to M2 as the *Post* and the Fed would have liked for America to believe. The *Post* had the temerity to write:

"It is the possible departure of M1 from this rebased (monitoring) M1 range that got the Treasury Department so concerned. In the one week that M1 fell below this range by about $1 billion, it was still more than $6 billion above the upper limits of the original range. Moreover, many observers, including some at the Fed, expect money growth to accelerate again soon."[33]

Paper Money Platitudes

Of course, it will accelerate again soon, so long as the Fed continues to print paper money without anything to back it up. The $6 billion that so surprised the *Washington Post* (if it was in fact a surprise) was nothing more than a massive printing of paper money by the Federal Reserve and had absolutely nothing to do with all the hocus-pocus talk about M1 and M2 and the public moving deposits from one to another for better interest rates. The *Post* story about the booming money supply, which never mentioned printing more paper money, concluded with this:

"The important question for the future is whether some more stable relationship will be re-established between money growth and economic growth. The Fed continues to hope that will be the case, while pursuing a highly judgmental approach to monetary policy, including keeping a close eye on the real economy."[34]

All that is smokescreen and double-talk by the Fed and its *Washington Post* mouthpiece. No "stable relationship" between money growth and the economy will ever be achieved by the Federal Reserve. It has been committed for years to follow whatever liberal economic political fad was popular at the moment so long as it could continue printing paper money at unprecedented levels.

Prevailing Politics

Robert J. Samuelson, who writes an economic column for *National Journal* that appears weekly in *The Washington Post*, had this to say about the Fed in a review of a new book while quoting author Maxwell Newton:

"The Fed is the power center that controls the American economy. The Fed is nominally independent from the White House and, if technically accountable to Congress, does little more than report its activities. The Fed is, in fact, the classic embodiment of the independent authority which, shielded from direct political pressures and managed by non-political appointees, is supposed to govern in the 'public interest.'"

All this is widely believed, but incorrect, according to Samuelson, who goes on to comment:

"Wrong, not because the people who run the Fed are unconcerned with the public interest. Not because they are political puppets. In general, the people who run the Fed have been technocrats—economists and bankers for the most part. And they have generally striven to 'do good', in the best sense of the word. The fact is that few institutions involved in matters so sensitive and central to politics can hold themselves above politics. The Fed, for one, does not. It has adapted to the prevailing political climate. The central question is whether there is a better way to regulate the nation's money and credit markets than this pattern of haphazard political accommodation."[35]

And the central point to this central question, Samuelson might have added, is that the Fed persists in printing bales of paper money to meet whatever political need arises at the time.

Washington Post Power

We call the *Washington Post* the mouthpiece of the Federal Reserve—and Wall Street—because it is still owned and published by the heirs of Eugene Meyer, Jr. Meyer was an heir of old-line international bankers and an international gold dealer with his partner Bernard Baruch. His father was a partner in Lazard Freres, international banking house of Paris and New York. Meyer and Baruch purchased the Alaska-Juneau gold mine in 1915. When Baruch helped finance Woodrow Wilson's campaign for president, Wilson rewarded him and his partner Meyer with appointments to key financial posts in the Wilson administration that allowed them to profit from World War I. Baruch was named chairman of the War Industries Board and a member of the Munitions Price Fixing Committee, and Meyer was appointed chairman of the War Finance Committee, responsible for disposing of some $2 billion worth of government securities to pay for the war. He not only administered their sale but dealt in them himself, capitalizing on his official position and inside information.

It was not until Herbert Hoover appointed Meyer to the Federal Reserve Board in 1931 that Meyer's dealing in World War I securities and Liberty Bonds, for which he was officially responsible, was revealed. The Senate hearing into his confirmation revealed he had duplicated $24 million in government bonds for reasons of his own and also had secretly destroyed

$10 billion in bonds for reasons known only to him and his administration. Such duplicity and secrecy and conflict of interest did not prevent Senate confirmation of his appointment to the Fed.[36]

Meyer bought the then financially-ailing *Washington Post* in 1933 so he and his Wall Street associates would have a newspaper voice in the nation's capital. The *Post* was never a very good paper under Meyer's direction; but it developed perhaps the best editorial page, although traditionally left-of-center, in the country, which was all Meyer was interested in. He wanted to speak to the president and Congress daily through his editorial page to influence and dictate public policy in his own interest. Although he resigned from the Fed board in 1935, Meyer continued as an official of the New Deal's Reconstruction Finance Corporation through which he had control over some $2 billion in federal funds to loan. Although it was all paper money, Meyer, nevertheless, had power over who would succeed and who would fail during the Depression years.

The Red Bed

Meyer hired as his chief editorial writer the self-proclaimed libertarian journalist Alan Barth and gave him a free hand to promote all his liberal views. This resulted in the *Post* defending Earl Browder, then head of the Communist Party in America in 1950, along with communist agents Alger Hiss and Harry Dexter White, when they were exposed. The *Post* led the relentless attack on Senator Joe McCarthy and also on the House committee on Un-American Activities. It put the *Post* in bed with the communists, and it has never quite been able to shake off the partnership.

The subscribers and advertisers of Washington, D.C., didn't take to the *Post* until well after World War II when Meyer's personable but emotionally unstable son-in-law, Phil Graham, succeeded him as publisher. Meyer, whose personal fortune was more than $60 million, lost $1 million a year or more on the *Post* the first 20 years that he owned it.

Meyer's daughter, Katherine Graham, succeeded her husband as publisher after his mental illness destroyed him; and she became more than ever the voice of Wall Street, much to the dismay of the *Post* staff that had gained such notoriety during the Watergate story.

As David Halberstam reported in his book about the news media, *The Powers That Be, Washington Post*, reporters thought they had been working for a traditionally liberal institution: "...an institution that regularly dictated the humane, honorable solution to the conflicts of other institutions, but was now a liberal institution that followed the norms of Wall Streets; and Wall Street was not necessarily committed to humane, honorable solutions."[37]

What "Wall Street" was committed to, through operation of the Federal

Reserve, was enriching itself through manipulation of inflationary paper money as fast as it could be printed.

Money Monopoly

Paper money is political money, not real money. Despite the "reason" for creating a so-called "independent" Federal Reserve so it would supposedly be free of partisan politics, it has, in fact, been the political tool of the world's big money lenders, the bankers. Morgan and his associates saw early on that monopolies of mere railroads and steel and oil and rubber trusts were nothing compared with a *monopoly on money*. Link control of money with an income tax and you have all of society working for you instead of vice versa with a monopoly or trust. Think about that!

That's what the Federal Reserve is all about. That's what the Federal Reserve set out to do—destroy the old dollar values based on gold or silver and substitute unlimited printing of worthless paper money based on nothing but the printing press upon which they are run. Control of the printing press through the Federal Reserve would assure unlimited printing of money, and a federal income tax would assure a *cash flow* on which unlimited credit (national debt) could be *pyramided*.

This is the most ingenious scheme or scam for *stealing money* ever devised! Take the gold and silver out of circulation, flood the economy with paper money backed by the income tax sweat of the working public, and you soon have taken their goods and given them paper for them. As long as the suckers think the paper is worth something, why not? They can't cash it for gold or silver. As more and more of it is printed, it becomes less and less valuable, meaning prices will go up until, ultimately, a wheelbarrow of it will be needed to buy a loaf of bread.

This is why automobile prices have caused "sticker shock" the past few years when prospective buyers see a little tin can on wheels that costs more than a Cadillac or Lincoln cost before the Fed started destroying the dollar at a rapid rate in 1971. This is why bread costs $1 a loaf some places. This is why utility rates have gone up and payrolls have shut down, causing America's present high rate of unemployment.

It can all be blamed on the mad printing of paper money by the Federal Reserve, printing necessitated in part by the just-as-insane limitless spending of a big federal government of money it does not have, never has had and never will have. The spending is tacked on the far end of the federal deficit.

This is why politicians call for more taxes, not to use the money to spend but just to pay interest on the $1 trillion dollar national debt headed for $3 trillion by the year 2000. And we don't "owe it to ourselves," we owe it to the owners of the Bank for International Settlements and the bank's foreign banking associates who—make no mistake about it—dictate monetary policy to the Federal Reserve. And that policy is to do just what it has been doing since it was created—print more and more paper money for the American people until the American economy is ruined because there is so much of it floating around and it is so worthless.

When that happens is the WHEN James Paul Warburg was talking about one-world government taking over. We will owe it to them.

Chapter 3

Fed Confetti: FUNNY, PHONY MONEY

"Always Good"

On the island of Yap in the southwest Pacific Ocean the natives use large wheel-shaped stones for money. The stones range in size from one foot to eight feet in diameter and have holes in the center of them so they can be carried on poles. Each stone is valuable and together they constitute a big part of the island's wealth. They aren't used for everyday transactions but they are used for the larger ones—like buying a bride or a herd of cattle or a grove of coconut palms. For more routine transactions, the natives use mother-of-pearl and tridacana shells.

The large stones are valuable to Yap natives because a great deal of labor must be exerted to get them. The stones are not quarried on Yap but on an island some forty miles across the sea. The old tradition for a young man who wanted a bride was to pay the father of the bride (her price based on social status) with one of the stones. To get one, he had to round up all his friends and family he could who were willing, and they set out for the far island in outrigger canoes. Once there, they quarried the stone, moved it to the beach, loaded it on lashed-together outriggers, took it back forty miles across open water to Yap and unloaded it on the beach there. The many stones on Yap are well-known to the natives, and they can change hands frequently as a medium of exchange or store of value without changing location.

The Yap experience with modern currencies illustrates why the odd stones have retained their value through the centuries and also why some people in the world accumulate and rely upon gold today. Spain first claimed Yap by discovery in the sixteenth century, and Spanish money was installed as the currency. After Spain's defeat in the Spanish-American War, Yap was sold to Germany in 1899, and German currency was installed on Yap. When Germany was defeated in World War I,

57

Yap was transferred as a League of Nations mandate to Japan in 1920, and Japanese currency was the order for Yap. After Japan's defeat in World War II, the United Nations transferred Yap to the United States as a trust territory, and U.S. currency has been used there since 1947.

When U.S. money was first introduced to Yap, an elderly Yap chief remarked, "First Spanish money no good, then German money no good, then Japanese money no good. Yap money always good!"[1]

The Meaning of Money

The Yap Island money stones, called *fei*, incidentally, raise the question of just what is money and how is it used? Basically, money is an item, a thing, that people accept as payment for goods or services. Whatever serves as money, whether it is Yap stones or American paper dollars, must be acceptable to those who are exchanging it on markets. So anything acceptable has the potential to serve as money.

In simple or primitive societies, market exchanges often are made by barter—the exchange of one good for another without the use of money as a go-between. In military prison camps, cigarettes have been used for money. In Zaire in Africa, a tribe of pygmy hunters trade ivory from elephant tusks for metal used in making their metal-tipped arrows and also for some agricultural goods. Money is not needed there because they trade basically in the number of arrow tips per ivory tusk. Barter is fine, as far as it goes, when there exists a double coincidence of wants. But the more complicated a society becomes, the less able barter is to accommodate trades in the market. So an alternative to barter must be found, and for centuries this has taken the form of currencies of various substance and value.

Money is used as a low-cost way of facilitating the distribution of goods that complex societies produce and distribute. The problem with money is that it has for centuries had a tendency to become inflated because governments issue more of it than they have gold, silver or anything else of value to back it up. Governments always have been the worst debasers of money.

Whatever is used for money should not be confused with the actual functions of money. Whether stones, cigarettes, arrow tips, ivory, gold, silver or paper, the thing or things being used as money should have the following characteristics:

It must serve as a medium of exchange by allowing people to exchange goods and services for it.

It must be a standard of value by which goods and services can be readily compared.

It must be a standard of debt allowing borrowers and lenders to specify how a debt can be repaid in a representation of purchasing power rather than in barter goods.

It must be a store of purchasing power, meaning it can be held until the holder is ready to spend it and can still be assured at that later time the money will be worth approximately what it was worth when he first got it.

It should be easily transferable, relatively scarce for value, portable for usefulness, durable, acceptable, recognizable and generally uniform in appearance. The currency also should be easily divisible for use and convenience in small transactions, much more easily divisible than, say, Yap stones or diamonds. If "money," whatever it is being used, has all those qualities and features, then it meets the major criteria of value and is considered a proper currency.[2]

The Trouble With Money

The trouble with money in America today is that the Federal Reserve, which issues the currency and exercises control over the amount in circulation and is obligated by law to report periodically how much is circulating for general use, no longer can *define money*. Therefore, the Fed's reports are basically *meaningless* and more *misleading* than they are helpful. The Federal Reserve has several different definitions of money, and by the time all of them are counted and totalled up, it is discovered that there are yet other kinds of "money" the Fed hasn't counted on.

Generally, the Fed has money classified in various forms of "M" (for money) such as:

M1, immediately spendable money like currency, checkable deposits, and traveler's checks in the hands of the public.

M2, a broader definition of the money supply including M1 plus non-checkable savings deposits and money market mutual fund shares.

M3, an even broader definition including M2 plus certificates of deposit and certain other highly liquid assets.

L (for liquid assets), a yet broader measure of liquid assets including M3 and even more forms of increasingly complex financial assets.[3]

With all that, there are still such things as credit cards, Eurodollars, Special Drawing Rights, electronic transfers and other new technological methods of "money" exchange which defy classification by the Fed. The truth is, the way the Federal Reserve operates, it doesn't know what money is anymore and can't define it. *It is basically in the business of printing paper money.*

The American dollar used to be called "good as gold" and things of quality were described as "sound as a dollar," but no more. There are so many paper dollars floating around, without anything to back them but the alleged faith and credit of the government, that they have become *cheap*. It takes more of them than it used to in order to buy anything. That's inflation and it's caused purely and simply by too much cheap, and perhaps worthless, paper money in circulation. Instead of curbing it, the government encourages the Federal Reserve to print more and more of it to pay for the many political promises the government has made over the years and is expected to deliver, whether it can afford to or not. That's what causes national debt, now well over $1.4 trillion dollars, including an annual federal budget deficit of $200 billion a year—or $200,000,000,000.00.

Heaven Help the Dollar!

Some Americans got excited about reports late in 1983 that the American dollar was reaching record highs compared with other major world currencies, trading profitably against the British pound, the French franc, the Italian lira, the Dutch guilder and the West German mark. It must be remembered that those currencies are in even worse shape than the American dollar, if the dollar trades well against them—meaning they, too, are over-printed, variegated paper of government offices, representing not wealth or gold or productivity, but merely politically motivated government printing orders.[4]

If the inflated American paper dollar issued by the Federal Reserve was valuable in trading against the currencies of our major allies in late 1983, heaven help Western Civilization!

And only heaven can help Western Civilization survive in its epic struggle with Satanic communism. People don't really believe in the dollar anymore because they don't believe in man's ability to act rationally anymore. This is not a by-product, but perhaps the major product, of the alleged new age of science under the influence of Darwin, Hegel, Marx and Engels, Nietzsche, Sartre, Mao and all the other humanist thinkers who have led much of the world to place man above God. They tried to teach us that man, rational thinking man, could do anything...could control his destiny. And he could, if he were perfect, but there was only one perfect man on this earth, Jesus Christ, and He was crucified by non-believers. However, "death could not hold its prey." He arose!

Man's imperfection includes covetousness and greed. That's what destroyed the old, more moral way of doing things and led to the financial chaos that the United States and the rest of the world find themselves in today.

Few people know this, certainly the press hasn't publicized it, but it was a financial scheme of communist Russia that blasted America financially and dragged us down from world leader to just another country struggling to survive financially.

Newton and His Apple

Here is the story:

It started with Sir Isaac Newton—scientific genius, explainer of gravity, developer of calculus, analyzer of the laws of motion, author of *Principia*, expert in optics, one of the world's leading certified thinkers. Because of his prestige, his political affiliation and his money, he was appointed Master of the Mint of Great Britain in 1717. As Adam Smith said, "maybe" he got hit on the head by an apple; but for whatever reason, he declared—as Master of the Mint—the stabilization of English currency by announcing a new standard monetary unit that would be guaranteed by the government—a gold coin called the guinea, so named because the gold in it came from the African colony of Guinea. It was worth twenty-one shillings and had 129.4 grams of gold in it. For nearly 100 years it was the key currency of the British Empire and the rest of the world. Basic monetary values everywhere were measured against the British guinea.

After the Napoleonic wars, the guinea became the British pound sterling, rounded off in value at twenty shillings and so named because the silver (Britain went to bimetallism after the Napoleonic wars), first arriving to be minted into coins based on the pound, was stamped "Easterling," the name of an Estonian banking house dealing in and shipping silver. The Britons, in their use of the King's English, merely shortened it to sterling. For another 100 years, the British pound sterling was the key currency of the Empire and the world until England sacrificed its wealth, its empire and a generation of young men in World War I. The British sent their gold and silver to America to pay for munitions and other war supplies. They issued bales of paper money, pound notes and the like to keep their economy, and that of the empire, going. When the war was over, the balance of financial power had shifted from Great Britain to the United States.

The British tried to maintain the traditional value of the pound at $4.86 in American dollars through the 1920s, but the strain of the war on the economy proved too much. The issuance of so much paper money undermined the pound, and the stock market crash and collapse of world credit in 1929-30 ended the 213-year reign of the British guinea and pound as the world's key currency. In 1931 the British severed the official tie of the pound and gold to let the pound "float" on the world currency market, meaning a pound was no longer worth $4.86 but was worth whatever buyers and sellers of the pound decided it was worth. The world no longer had a key currency.

The pound is dying hard. By 1940 it was still worth $4.03. After World War II, it was devalued in 1949 and was worth $2.80. In recent years, it has fluctuated as low as $1.80. So, when financial page headlines declare that the American dollar is "Soaring to Record Highs Against Major World Currencies," it only means that those paper currencies are only sinking lower in value because the governments issuing them are just like our Federal Reserve—unable to resist printing free money backed by nothing. *It does not mean that the dollar has increased in value.* =

The Floating Dollar

Just as the British cut loose the pound from gold in 1931 and let it "float" against the value of other world currencies, President Richard Nixon did the same thing with the American dollar in 1971, ending its brief reign as successor to the British guinea-pound as the world's key currency. Oh, the dollar is still the "measure" by which other currencies are evaluated, and the American dollar is the common denomination of money in most international transactions, but it no longer is the key currency dominating world markets.

In the financial chaos following World War I—the madness of German reparations payments expectations, the failure of the stock markets and credit, the Depression, the founding of the Bank for International Settlements—the American dollar reluctantly became the world's key currency because there was no other currency in shape to do it.

It became official near the end of World War II when the major allied nations agreed to the dollar as the key currency at the Bretton Woods, New Hampshire, Economic Summit in 1944 in which the post-war world economy was outlined. Representing the United States at Bretton Woods were communist agents Alger Hiss of the State Department and Harry Dexter White of the Treasury Department. They, along with the British sexual deviate and spendthrift economist, John Maynard Keynes, assured the eventual failure of the agreement, largely by insisting upon establishment of an International Monetary Fund and a World Bank to be administered by the United Nations, which soon would be under communist domination.

In those days the dollar was still convertible into gold—not by U.S. citizens, of course, but by any foreign nation which accumulated dollars, and there were many of them around the world due to the war and foreign aid.

American paper dollars flooded the world to finance post-war reconstruction, the revival of world trade, and the stationing of American troops overseas. And the paper came flooding back home to be exchanged for gold, something of far greater value than the Federal Reserve confetti in the minds of foreigners, if not Americans.

Counterfeiting for Communism

Vast amounts of paper money—no one knows how much—were printed by the Soviet Union at the end of World War II when Secretary of the Treasury Henry Morgenthau, Jr. and his aides, Harry Dexter White and Harold Glasser, supplied the communists with U.S. Treasury money engraving plates along with at least three airplane loads of proper ink and four airplane loads of authorized paper. The money printed with these plates was used to pay two years in salaries to communist soldiers occupying East Germany and other parts of Eastern Europe under communist domination. How much more has been counterfeited with the plates is not known to us.[6]

President Franklin D. Roosevelt had to have known about this operation and authorized it. Roosevelt had done a great deal of business with Morgenthau's father in the 1920s. Morgenthau, Jr. was a neighbor of Roosevelt at Hyde Park—a kind of gentleman farmer, having inherited his father's fortune. Morgenthau had never "worked" for a living beyond administering his inheritance, but was widely quoted for this April, 1944, saying at the Bretton Woods monetary conference:

"Prosperity has no fixed limits. It is not a finite substance to be diminished by division. On the contrary, the more of it that other nations enjoy, the more each nation will have for itself."

So the Morgenthau-White team gave the Russian communists U.S. Treasury engraving plates; and at Bretton Woods, it was White, Morgenthau's chief adviser, who drafted the plan for the International Monetary Fund that today drains more of the West's economic wealth into the communist bloc and the Third World.

White was a supposed expert on international economics at the Treasury, having business and economics degrees from Columbia, Stanford and Harvard. Morgenthau once said of him: "He can be disagreeable, quick-tempered, overly ambitious; and power goes to his head." Dean Acheson, a Wall Street financier who later was Secretary of State for President Truman, said he was "outraged by Harry White's capacity for rudeness in discussion." But White's alleged brilliance and intellect, and his influence with Morgenthau and Roosevelt, cloaked him with rarely-challenged authority.[7]

Morgenthau, White, Glasser and Alger Hiss loosed the flood of American paper money throughout the world, every dollar of it, at that time, redeemable in gold *for foreigners only.*

Looting Fort Knox

The Bretton Woods agreement was doomed to failure because the communists, Hiss and White, knew that men everywhere were greedy, faulty, often acted irrationally, and could not be trusted to confine themselves within a bargain. Nations could not politically adjust themselves to face economic reality when printing free paper money was so easy. The worst offender in this debasement of coin of the realm was the United States of America. American trade and payment deficits based on the paper dollar cried out for a devaluation of the dollar, but it was politically impossible in the U.S.A. at the time, and the dollar became greatly over-valued, setting it up for a crisis. In addition, nations of the world were *looting Fort Knox* by trading in the paper dollars for gold through the London Gold Pool, established in 1961 to hold down the price of gold by the U.S., Great Britain, West Germany, Switzerland, Belgium, Italy, and the Netherlands.

What this "pool" really amounted to was an instrument for emptying Fort Knox, robbing America of its gold and leaving the Americans holding a bag full of paper dollars which daily were becoming worth less and less as the Federal Reserve presses printed more and more of them.

Having looted the American gold, the gold pool was disbanded in 1968. The English pound was immediately devalued. The French franc was devalued in 1969. The German mark was devalued in 1970, and the American dollar was left hanging high and dry, all alone in the never-never land of paper money dreams.[8]

A temporary effort known as the Smithsonian Agreement failed to save Bretton Woods and the American dollar because the communists invented the so-called Eurodollars, which are nothing more than homeless American dollars still floating around the world currency exchanges that have not been turned in for gold. They can't now, because there is no more gold. In hindsight, it seems amazing no one thought of the Eurodollar sooner, but the Eurodollar scheme hatched in Moscow was planned and timed perfectly to destroy the remaining value of the dollar throughout the world and throw capitalist finance into chaos.

The Russian Ripoff

After the Hungarian revolt of 1956 was crushed by the Soviets under the leadership of then Soviet ambassador to Hungary, Yuri Andropov (later to become premier) the Soviets moved what American dollars they had out of New York banks into a Soviet-owned London bank, the Moscow Narodny Bank, for fear the Americans might freeze Soviet assets during the Cold War (as we did Iran's during the 1979-80 hostage crisis).

While other countries were turning in their American paper dollars for gold, the Soviets took theirs out of the U.S. and established an $800,000 account in their London bank. Within a year, the $800,000 was loaned out and repaid beyond the reach of the American banking system and the Federal Reserve. The Soviet-owned bank in Paris took some of the loan. The bank is named Bank Commercial pour l'Europe du Nord, and its cable address is Eurobank. The American dollars it loaned were soon called Eurodollars because of the cable address of the lending bank of their origin.

The financial attractiveness of the Eurodollar was not that it could be cashed for gold in America—which it could eventually anyway—but that it was an unregulated currency once outside the United States, beyond any mandatory or imposed interest rate ceilings or reserve requirements. In the U.S., the Federal Reserve controls currency through mandatory bank reserve requirement or interest rate ceilings. It couldn't do that with the Eurodollar beyond its reach and in the hands of foreigners. **It represented taxation without representation!**

Now borrowers, who used to go hat in hand to Washington or New

York for dollars and promise to meet Federal Reserve standards to get a U.S. loan, could instead get uncontrolled Eurodollars from banks in Canada or France or London or Switzerland or Italy or even the London Moscow Narodny Bank, when it was in Moscow's interest to loan American dollars. American banks quickly established branches in London to get in on the free-wheeling Eurodollar market, unshackled by the Federal Reserve. If the Fed tried to penalize them at home, the American bankers argued that if they couldn't do business in Eurodollars, then all the business would go to Germans or the French or the Swiss or the Italians or the British or, heaven forbid, the Russians.[9]

The Eurodollars boom came on the heels of the abandonment of the London gold pool because there had been a depletion of gold at Fort Knox anyway, and the only way the growing American balance of deficit payments to the rest of the world could be utilized was to deal in the free and easy atmosphere of Eurodollars paid for by the American government borrowing itself (that is, the taxpayers for the next few generations) into a deeper and deeper financial hole. What began with the $800,000 Soviet loan now amounts to a Eurodollar currency of nearly $1 trillion, all of which is the responsibility of the American taxpayer, thanks to the Federal Reserve printing press.[10]

Nixon, for all his faults, was no fool about money. He knew there was no gold in any sufficient quantity left to pay for the Eurodollars should they someday come home. In 1971, he cut the dollar loose from gold, backing out of the Bretton Woods-Smithsonian currency agreements, ending the dollar's reign as the world key currency and throwing the American economy onto the mercy of the rest of the world's sharp traders, including those operating the Bank for International Settlements in Switzerland. Our financial destiny was no longer our own. We had overspent ourselves with cheap paper money into the debt of the rest of the world.

Now the markets—meaning the flood of paper money in the world (mostly American paper dollars, Federal Reserve confetti)—are bigger than banks. They (we're talking about the money market controllers, the owners of the international banks led by the Bank for International Settlements in Switzerland) sniff around the various national paper currencies like dogs over an assortment of bones, seeking the one that might be most profitable for the moment. Some days the dollar fares well against other currencies; some days it doesn't. It's beyond our control now. *We had our shot as world financial kingpin and blew it by printing too much paper money.*

The Housing Hedge

Intelligent, perceptive Americans began years ago to see this, to see what has happened, and are running from the paper American dollar. They don't want dollars in their pockets because the dollar is worth less every day. They want to convert the paper dollars into something of value. The most stable investment that most Americans have found for their paper dollars is real estate, principally their residence, because it (1) meets a need as everyone has to have someplace to live and (2) has been appreciating in value generally since the Depression, outstripping inflation in some hot spots like Southern California where $100,000 houses are considered cheap and $1 million houses are becoming ever more commonplace. And these are not necessarily new houses or mansions. Some of them are houses forty years old that have been "modernized" with new plumbing and wiring, expanded closet space, a hot tub and a tennis court—all to hike their real estate value in the modern market.

The residential real estate market is based on *government policy* established by the 1934 Depression era National Housing Act that set up the Federal Housing Administration (FHA) and has been followed by many other housing laws strengthening the policy. This policy amounts to a huge *government subsidy* for homeowners, paid for, naturally, with paper dollars rolled off the Federal Reserve presses. The government wants each American to buy a house and provides a *quadruple subsidy* for those who do. If you buy a house you can:

1. Deduct the interest on the mortgage from your income tax.
2. Deduct the real estate taxes.
3. Legally avoid tax payments on the profits from selling a house.
4. Get a long-term mortgage that makes home-owning as cheap monthly as renting, up until about 1980 when fixed-term mortgages began being replaced with variable or negotiable mortgages.

The government's housing policy is based on the printing of cheap paper money. People wanted and demanded decent housing they couldn't afford, and the government made it possible by financing the housing with subsidies based on paper money.

It has been a great free ride, but now it is about over because greed in the form of speculation is putting an end to it, and people are wising up to the true value of paper money.

The housing boom should collapse economically because of the paper money, but the government cannot afford to let it collapse. The housing industry's political constituency is too big—not just contractors and building materials suppliers but also some 86 million houses and 56 million homeowners expected to nearly double in number by the 1990s. Is the government going to stand by and let them be thrown into the street when they can no longer pay their mortgages? Not if it wants to survive politically and avoid revolution. And not as long as there is still paper and ink with which to print more money.[11]

Bondage in Bonds

How can the government get away with having the Federal Reserve print this seemingly endless supply of virtually worthless paper money based on nothing?

Here is how:

When the government decides it needs more money, which is all the time, it orders its fiscal agent, the United States Treasury, to print up some *United States Bonds*. No matter that the bonds are based on nothing but paper. The government issues them on faith—fiat bonds, based on its faith that American taxpayers will be suckers enough to continue paying taxes far into future generations to supposedly support these bonds and that taxpayers will continue to honor the credit of the government. *Faith and credit*. That's what the American currency system and economy are based on—faith and credit. The bonds are nothing more than a government IOU.

The U.S. Bonds are then sent to the Federal Reserve, GIVEN to the Federal Reserve, in return for an amount of currency printed and coined equal to the amount of the bonds in that particular bond issue.

The Federal Reserve's worthless paper money and cheap small coinage is then distributed through federal expenditures and through the Federal Reserve Banking System. The government has declared this worthless money, based on nothing but faith and credit, to be "legal tender," meaning the government will accept it for taxes and that, in the government's opinion (the federal courts), it also is good for the payment of private debts.[12]

Making Money With Mirrors

Once this paper money is in the hands of the banks, where most of it usually goes sooner or later in the form of deposits, it has a "magic" and highly inflationary way of multiplying itself known to economists and bankers as the *deposit multiplier principle*. The deposit multiplier is a money-making conspiracy of big bankers in cahoots with the Federal Reserve and the Treasury Department to produce money by bookkeeping backed up by more U.S. bonds and Fed confetti.

It works like this:

The history of banking shows that everyone who has money on deposit doesn't demand it back at once except in case of manias or panics. They prefer to draw interest on it when they are not using it. So banks loan it out at even greater interest to make profit on it. But they can't loan it all out, so they must, by law, keep some of it on hand to pay those depositors who do come in wanting their money. The deposits on hand are known in banking and Federal Reserve terminology as the required reserve or fractional reserve. The Federal Reserve Board determines what percentage of deposits must be held. That way, the Fed can make money loose or tight by raising or lowering the reserve requirement. In our illustration, let's say the reserve requirement is twenty percent.

Mr. Depositor enters the bank with a government tax refund check for $5,000 and deposits it to his account. Mr. Borrower then borrows the $4,000 left after Mr. Banker takes out the twenty percent or $1,000 required reserve from Mr. Depositor's $5,000. So the $5,000 has doubled through the magic of bookkeeping to $10,000!

Count it. Mr. Depositor has $5,000 in his account. The bank has $1,000 in required reserve. Mr. Borrower just walked out with a $4,000 loan. Add it up. It comes to $10,000!

And it doesn't end there. Mr. Borrower goes out and buys a $4,000 camper cabin to put on the back of his pickup truck. The company he bought it from deposits the $4,000 in its bank account. The bank places twenty percent of the $4,000 in required reserve ($800) and loans out the remaining $3,200 to yet another borrower. This cycle is repeated until the original $5,000 has become $25,000! The extra $20,000 was created by the banks by just lending on their books what they call "excess reserves," knowing historically that all the depositors are not going to come back in at once demanding their money.

And what happens if they do, or if a great number of them do? That's where the Federal Reserve System comes in, the ostensible reason it was created. If a bank begins to run short of money, it calls up its regional Federal Reserve bank and merely orders more money. The Fed bank calls the Fed office in Washington for more money for all its branch banks needing it, and the Fed office simply calls the U.S. Treasury and orders—yes, orders—another *U.S. bond* sent over in the total amount needed by all twelve of the regional Fed banks so that the Fed can print and coin the currency—using the Treasury's Bureau of Engraving to do so.[13]

The Perfect Scam

Is this a perfect scam or what? Wonder of wonders, money from nowhere! Send the bill, the U.S. bond, the government's IOU now held by the Federal Reserve and its international banker owners, to the present and future generations of U.S. taxpayers.

This is the greatest system of counterfeiting and robbery ever devised. The government robs its own people through this system of debased currency, scatters some of it back to the masses through social largesse to curb social unrest or revolution, and feeds the rest of it through international banks and multi-national business firms into the Eurodollars and other foreign currency markets to be controlled by those interests dominating the Bank for International Settlements, where our Fed chairman is not really a member of the board of directors but merely an observer, and sometimes consultant, when called on. Unbelievable? You had better believe it, because it's true! It has just been covered up in economic doubletalk and deliberate distortion of facts by the financiers, politicians and news media insiders who have known all along what's going on but dared not tell the public. As Ripley would say, "believe it or not!"

Enough people are beginning to believe it, or else they wouldn't be fleeing from the American paper dollar. Americans have created a big business boom of their own by converting their paper dollars into real estate, gold, stocks and bonds, money market mutual funds, commodities, art, Chinese porcelain, antiques, condominiums, silver, futures speculations, jewels, furs, Las Vegas and Atlantic City gambling, lottery tickets—anything but paper dollars.

Constitutional Money: Gone With the Wind

Back when the government was in the money business, before it abdicated its responsibility to the Federal Reserve, its authority was based on Article 1, Section 8, of the U.S. Constitution which says, "The Congress shall have the power to coin money, regulate the value thereof, and of foreign coin, and fix the standard of weights and measures."

Here we see Sir Isaac Newton's contribution to sound currency again, by having fixed the weight and measure of the guinea in 1717 to prevent it from being debased by the government or anyone else. The guinea rivaled the Spanish doubloon and other world coins which had a true weight and measure of gold or silver in them. Sir Isaac's 129.4 grams of gold prescribed for the guinea meant just that, and anyone could weigh it or measure it to see if it had sufficient gold in it and that it had not been "clipped" or "shaved" by previous holders of the coin, some of whom were not above taking a kind of royalty from each coin passing through their hands by clipping or shaving a slight amount of gold or silver off of it to be melted down later into bullion.

Sir Isaac's system of weight and measure for a coin was an honest one, and it found its way into the U.S. Constitution some sixty years later. That's what the "standard of weights and measures" phrase in the Constitution means. It's not talking about weighing and measuring meat or wheat; it's talking about metallic coins and their true content.

As for the "foreign coin" phrase, the Constitution was written at a time when foreign coinage was common and acceptable as currency in the former British colonies that became the new American republic. In those days such foreign coins as the British guinea, Spanish doubloons and silver dollars, Portuguese "Joes," Brazilian coins, French crowns and livres—and later the metallic coins of the former Spanish colonies in Latin America—circulated freely in the United States and largely were acceptable as currencies in business. So regulating their value in relation to American coinage was a Constitutional duty of Congress, and it would be easy to do so long as everyone was honest and the coins were full-bodied metal as their mints had issued them.

But men are imperfect, as are the governments they create, and they sin by cheating. Debasing coinage by passing it off at something less than the true value it was intended to convey is a profitable sin. This has culminated in the American paper dollar, or more accurately, the Federal Reserve Note. The Constitution has gone with the wind, in the name of progress.

In the name of progress, the money changers and profiteers of this world long ago abandoned balanced budgets, both nationally and personally, for deficit spending. In so doing, they abandoned honest money and honest currency, exchanging it for debt or misbegotten profit.

The opening phrase of the Constitutional mandate to Congress empowers it "to coin money, regulate the value thereof..." It says nothing about Congress making money or creating money or turning over its Constitutional responsibility for coining money to anyone or any other institution. The intent was for the Congress to take gold and silver and turn them into money by making coins out of them. That's what money was in those days. All so-called "paper money" was supposed to be nothing more than a warehouse receipt for precious metal in storage.

What's "Money" Worth?

The original American $20 gold piece was an ounce of gold. That's what the South African one-ounce Krugerrand is today, only it is not marked with a denominational value. It speaks for itself, whatever the world value of gold. The American $20 gold piece, at this writing, would be worth approximately $400, probably much more because of its numismatic collector's value and the gold premium extracted by dealers.

An old silver quarter contained .1808 ounces of silver (thanks to the Sir Isaac-Constitutional intent), which meant it had an intrinsic value of slightly more than 24 cents. That was back before the Congress turned over American money to the Federal Reserve, which began over-issuing and counterfeiting coins and paper money. With silver in the approximate range of $10 an ounce at this writing, the old silver quarter is now worth $1.80. Today's modern quarter issued by the Federal Reserve through the Treasury mints contains no silver and only about a penny's worth of copper. Even if copper increased 500 percent in value (and it has been steady at about 80 cents per pound for years), the modern quarter would still have only about five cents worth of metal in it.[14]

In a U.S. Mint comparison of old silver coins compared with newer coins clad in nickel alloy, discontinued silver coins were about 90 percent silver and 10 percent copper; whereas, the new coins were 91.67 percent copper and 8.33 percent nicklel.

Their true worth stacked up like this in the study made in 1974 at 1974 values, and the discrepancy would be far greater in a current comparison:

The silver dollar, $3.54; the new nickel-clad "silver" dollar, four cents.

The half-dollar, $1.65; the new half-dollar, two cents.

The quarter, 83 cents; the new quarter, one cent.

The dime, 33 cents; the new dime, .04 cents.

It is interesting to note that the intrinsic value of the old silver dime was worth eight times as much as the new "silver" dollar. Even the old copper penny was reported to have .047 cents worth of copper in it then, which made it worth more than the new dime!

This is why old U.S. coins now out of circulation sell at such high prices among collectors or people simply looking for hedges against paper money and new coin inflation. The old coins had real gold and silver in them.

If a coin counterfeiter was arrested and put on trial today for making quarters with only ten cents worth of silver in them, he could probably claim in his defense that he was issuing more valuable coins than those currently being minted by the Federal Reserve. Even though his coins might be more valuable, the government prosecution would convict him for violating, if not the coinage, at least the coinage monopoly held by the Federal Reserve with the approval of Congress which passed the Federal Reserve Act in 1913. In other words, only the Federal Reserve has the right to counterfeit coins today.

Killing the Currency

The Federal Reserve's coinage operation, or manipulation, which is a better word for describing this rape of currency, not only violates the literal wording of the Constitution and its intent but also breaks the federal law in regard to fraud, calling for a fine of up to $10,000 and imprisonment for up to five years or both.[15]

The Federal Reserve is not minting and issuing coins; it is only passing off almost worthless tokens as coins. It would be more honest to manufacture plastic tokens like poker chips with their alleged value stated on them, as gambling casinos do, than to attempt to deceive the public with the counterfeit coins the Fed is now issuing as "money." If you look closely at any "silver" coin in circulation today you will see the copper inside it through its serrated edges. The "silver" covering is nothing but a practically worthless nickel-zinc alloy. The serrated edge, incidentally, is another deception. It was intended, originally, to prevent shaving or clipping of full-bodied coins of silver or gold. If the uniform serration was tampered with, it was obvious to the eye the coin had been shaved or clipped and did not contain its full value of precious metal. Today's copper-based coins are not worth shaving or clipping—or even melting down for bullion—with copper at 80 cents a pound, but the Federal Reserve retains serrated edging on most coins to continue the

71

deception of its rape of the currency.

The debasement of the currency by the Federal Reserve is as effective with paper money as it is with metal coinage. Gold and silver currency have the disadvantage of weight, especially in large sums, so the government—and later the Fed—printed paper money that could be substituted to represent gold and silver held in the national treasury. The paper money was supposed to be merely a receipt for precious metal on hand that would be paid to the bearer of the paper on demand.

The temptation was too much for the Federal Reserve profit makers. Before the Fed came into being in 1913, the government of the United States of America issued gold and silver certificates payable in gold or silver coin on demand. U.S. notes also were issued payable in a certain amount of dollars on demand. Gold certificates were issued from 1863 to 1928, when the last ones were printed; and they were withdrawn from circulation in 1934, when President Roosevelt took American citizens (but not foreign countries) off the gold standard. Silver certificates were issued from 1886 to 1963, when the last ones were printed; and they were taken out of circulation in 1968, the same time the last of silver coins with any true value of silver in them were removed from circulation.

Worthless Wording

As Federal Reserve notes replaced the certificates and U.S. notes, the wording on the face of the paper dollars also changed. The first and, at least, quasi-legitimate Federal Reserve notes issued from 1913 to 1934 included a "gold clause" which read, "Redeemable in gold on demand at the United States Treasury or in gold or lawful money at any Federal Reserve Bank."

That clause was removed from Fed notes issued after 1934, when the Gold Reserve Act made it illegal for Americans to own gold. The new clause said, "This note is legal tender for all debts public and private and is redeemable in lawful money at the United States Treasury or any Federal Reserve Bank."

The new clause declared Federal Reserve notes "legal tender" as a result of the Thomas Amendment to the Agricultural Adjustment Act of 1933 which said that all forms of currency and apparently even small change became "legal tender." And the "lawful money" statement declares that the Federal Reserve note itself is not lawful money but can be redeemed for lawful money, apparently meaning gold and silver certificates and U.S. notes; but no bank will give you any of those for a Federal Reserve note, no matter what it says. The Fed pulled a switcheroo on the American public and left us holding an IOU note that is not actually legal tender, despite its self-declaratory statement, and can't be redeemed anywhere for anything. *We got left holding the bag, but the Fed note is worth even less than a paper bag because there is not as much paper in it.*

The only value of this phony money is that it does state that the U.S. government will accept it for payment of taxes. That alone gives it credibility. People believe that they can at least pay taxes with it and, therefore, will accept it for money.

Another wording change on the present Federal Reserve note is that the words "pay to the bearer on demand" have been removed. The note can't be redeemed for anything, so it is a note to pay nothing. It claims to be legal "tender" for all debts public and private, but what, in fact, does it "tender"? Gold? Silver? Certificates for same? U.S. notes? No, it doesn't tender anything. Therefore, how can it be "legal"?

Its only actual value is that the government will accept it for taxes. If the government were to announce that from now on it would accept paper clips or pumpkins for taxes, Federal Reserve notes would lose what little value they have as tax instruments and be worth absolutely nothing. The U.S. Treasury no longer has anything to tender for Federal Reserve notes because far too many of them have been printed. A tender is something of good and valuable consideration. The government is bankrupt of anything good or valuable or legal, in regard to currency or specie.[16]

The old U.S. notes were first issued by the Lincoln administration to finance the Civil War after bankers tried to hijack the government by charging up to twenty-eight percent interest for their bank note loans. The war was an emergency, and millions of dollars worth of the U.S. "Greenbacks", as they were known, were issued. Later, when their value was tested in court, they were declared unconstitutional.[17]

It was only when the government made them redeemable in gold, effective January 1, 1879, that they were declared constitutional![18]

Corrupt Civilization Cited

It had been Lincoln's intention to redeem the "Greenbacks" in gold, and had he lived, it likely would not have taken so long. Lincoln's death was a tragedy in many ways, but Prince Otto Bismarck-Schonhausen, the chancellor of Germany, was most prophetic when he said, upon hearing of Lincoln's assassination:

"The death of Lincoln was a disaster for Christendom. There was no man in the United States great enough to wear his boots...I fear that foreign bankers with their craftiness and torturous tricks will entirely control the exuberant riches of America and use it to systematically corrupt modern civilization. They will not hesitate to plunge the whole of Christendom into wars and chaos in order that the earth should become their inheritance."[19]

As we have seen from our study of the Bank for International Settlements, the Federal Reserve and the phony money of the Fed, Bismarck was more prophetic than even he realized.

The total destruction of American money, as we knew it historically, is nearing completion. The Treasury Department, which does nothing without the consent of the Federal Reserve, announced in late 1983 that it is considering significant changes in American currency. Claiming it is concerned about the sophistication of modern photocopying machines that come very close to accurate counterfeiting, the Treasury was entertaining a plan to issue paper currency in different colors, resembling the European currency style. Within the Treasury, there was talk about making the paper bills in different sizes as well. To do so would violate the uniformity characteristic of money, but it probably makes little difference so long as the government is headed toward annual deficits of $200 billion. With a few thousand billion more paper dollars floating around, no one will want to counterfeit a paper bill, anyway, because there will be so many of them that they won't be worth anything. But if they do change the color, what would be more appropriate for the U.S. dollar than red ink?[20]

Society Minus Cash = ?

The Federal Reserve and the government are well aware that the day is near when no one is going to want any part of the cheap flood of paper money that has been issued without anything to support it. The Federal Reserve—through the banking system—and the government—by approval of the Universal Product Code—are in the process of preparing America for a cashless society to meet that day.

Banks throughout America are installing Electronic Funds Transfer (EFT) Systems. These systems, specifically designed computers to control all money, include automated teller machines in banks and shopping centers, the checkless "direct deposit" and the also checkless debit card. A high-powered public relations campaign and news media blitz are currently being used to sell these systems to the public as more convenient, safer and cheaper methods of banking transactions. These alleged benefits are offset by computer errors negating convenience, loss of privacy in exchange for "safety," and, in due time, new and higher transaction fees that will increase the cost of banking.

Millions of American employees already are being paid, not in cash or checks, but by "direct deposit" in which their pay is deposited to their accounts by computer without any actual cash or checks in the transaction. Social Security checks also are starting to be transferred directly by computer to the banks. "Direct deposit" is still voluntary but is expected to reach ninety percent participation in the 1990s, and, if it doesn't, it likely will be mandated by federal law dictated by the banking rulers.

When everyone's payroll is on banking-controlled and government-controlled computers, an individual's pay can be stopped by pushing a button, and his financial records will be readily accessible for examination by not only the Internal Revenue Service, but by any

other organization powerful enough to influence the government to let it examine the records.

It is ironic that this system of electronic funds transfer was already commonplace in 1984, the year of George Orwell's fictional book based on "Big Brother is watching" and provides the government a means of massive surveillance of the population.

Many banks are starting to issue statements produced by computer instead of returning cancelled checks. The next step is to persuade bank customers to stop writing checks altogether and begin using "debit cards" or electronic checks. Debit cards look like plastic credit cards but are, in fact, electronic checks. The difference is that, with a credit card, the purchaser does not have to have the money in the bank and is billed for the purchase later, with interest charges. A debit card requires that the money already be on deposit in the bank because the account is charged immediately for any purchase through the electronic funds transfer system.

The debit card has no name or address on it, only a bar code similar to those now found on most grocery store items which are checked by passing the bar code over an electronic beam at the checkout stand.

Identifying Marks

The bar codes now found on most merchandise are part of a government-approved Universal Product Code—a series of bars, lines and numerals providing identifying marks concerning the manufacturer, distributor, the product, its size, quantity, weight, if necessary, and price. Any kind of identification needed can be programmed into the Universal Product Code for each item.

The danger in the Electronic Funds Transfer-Universal Product Code system should be apparent. When universally installed, no one can be paid or can purchase anything unless their debit card is in order. If whoever controls this massive surveillance system decides an individual is out of step with society, he can be "unplugged" and left without funds and without access to the absolute necessities of life, to say nothing of luxuries.[21]

The single plastic debit card (or "credit card" as its proponents are still describing it) will soon replace most cash and all checks. The Rockefellers' Chase Manhattan Bank has installed 2,000 automated tellers in 47 states. Another 1,200 financial institutions with 15 million depositors belong to the same Chase system known as "Plus."

Mobil Oil is experimenting with a plastic card that pays for fuel automatically in Norfolk, Va. The card automatically deducts the cost from the cardholder's home checking account. In Florida, the Publix Super Markets chain has set up automatic tellers outside each store that can reach different bank systems, and the same debit card can also be used to buy groceries at the chain's checkout counters.

Hundreds of other banks and merchants are in a frantic technology overhaul to replace the inflated paper money with the electronic kind that no one can count except the central controller. Within the next few years, if not sooner, most purchases will be transacted with machines. Replacing cash, checks and charge plates will be one or two universal pieces of plastic with a personal code on it. The cardholder will place the card in a computer-controlled machine and push the debit button to have the price of a purchase automatically subtracted from his bank account or push the credit button to charge the purchase.

There are an estimated 40,000 teller machines already in place, and the number increases daily. About half of them are connected with one or more multi-bank networks, some of them national in scope. This technological revolution that will soon end the "cash and check system" that we know today is costing millions upon millions of dollars. It is considered to be worth it to the banks and to retailers that have found electronics save money in comparison with the cumbersome process of collecting and clearing checks, holding cash for armored car service transfer, and outmoded conventional bookkeeping.

Consumers seem to be readily adapting to the electronic money system even without sharing in the alleged cost savings resulting from automation. With cash registers that can read debit cards costing at least $1,500 each, we don't expect banks and merchants to pass on any savings in the near future, if ever.[22]

Your Final Number

The growing use of the Universal Products Code and the Electronic Funds Transfer System convinces some Bible prophecy students and teachers that the Biblical "666 System" they believe to be the "Mark of the Beast", mentioned in Revelation, is at hand. And not all of them are radical "nuts" either, like the conventional news media pretends to make them out. For example, one outspoken critic of the system is Mary Stewart Relfe, Montgomery, Alabama businesswoman who is also a pilot and a member of the Montgomery Aviation Authority. In her book, *When Your Money Fails...The 666 System is Here*, she publishes her research showing widespread commercial usage of the Biblical number 666 as the "Mark of the Beast" (Revelation 13:18) and comments on the increasing use of credit-debit cards:

"Soon you will receive a Final Card and a *Final Number*. It may be called a National Identity Card or a Registration Card or some other name. But it will be the card which will be as mandatory in distributing your earnings as the Social Security Card is now in earning your wages. It will be a card by which you both earn and distribute your income."[23]

Following Satan

Another prophetic writer and thinker on this subject is the Rev. Doug Clark of Orange, California, who says:

"Satan has subjugated the masses of the heathen world to his ideas. He also has succeeded in subjugating another one-third of the world to his communist plot of such a hideous nature. Russia, along with Eastern Europe, China and other oriental locations, is under the control of Satan through communism...

"Satan is using men to promote his financial conspiracy plot and by 'demonetizing gold and silver' will cause our currencies to fail in value and power and then bring about our fall to such an extent that we would have to *follow his ideas to recover.* If the Western nations crumble financially and economically, then we would be vulnerable to Satan's ideas on world finance such as will be presented through his man, the Antichrist, and the Mark of the Beast."[24]

Adoration of the *machine* since the start of the Industrial Revolution has led to degradation of man in the thoughts and eyes of secular humanists. They no longer believe that man is a creation of God but is merely an animal which has evolved from sub-species. The industrial-automation revolution, of which the computer is a major tool, is leading to the development of what scientists today are calling "artificial intelligence", or machines that think.

We are not against scientific development or machines that think, but we are against the control of them by evil forces that would use science, industrialization and automation to subdue mankind and make all people think and behave uniformly. God made human beings free to think individually and to act accordingly, even if they are wrong. God sacrificed His Son Jesus Christ so mankind's wrong-thinking sin would be forgiven when each man accepts Christ as his personal saviour. If Satan, through sinful man, were to gain control of the new industrial-automation revolution in technology to subjugate man to his will instead of God's will, then the final perversion of man would be complete.

Saving Ourselves

The Bible tells us that there is no power to save man from this, or any other dreadful fate, except God through His Son Jesus Christ.

Artificial or electronic intelligence, combined with mechanical creatures or robots that operate independently of humans, is bringing a revolutionary and unprecedented dimension to American life. It is good to have machines which can do jobs too dangerous for man, such as working inside nuclear reactors or mining precious metals in outer space; but the control of such machines, of such power, could be the key to survival.

We don't want to stray from our subject of money, but the development

77

and control of machines such as the automatic teller go a long way toward control of not only money but of mankind.[25]

Fruits of Liberty

One of the great economic thinkers of modern time, generally ignored by politicians, other economists and the news media people, who embraced the something-for-nothing economic philosophy of John Maynard Keynes, was the Austrian economist and teacher Ludwig Von Mises. Von Mises clearly saw the link between money, credit, machines and tyranny, more so than most other twentieth century economists who ignored political realities. Von Mises, in his classic work, *The Theory of Money and Credit*, said:

"The main political problem (of economics) is how to prevent the rulers from becoming despots and enslaving the citizenry they were meant to serve. Defense of the individual's liberty against the encroachment of tyrannical governments is the essential theme of the history of Western Civilization. The characteristic feature of the Occident is its people's pursuit of liberty, a concern unknown to orientals. All the marvelous achievements of Western Civilization are fruits grown on the tree of liberty."[26]

The liberty of Western Civilization is no accident. God caused it to happen and intended it that way. A monumental moment in world history that forever divided the ways of the Orient from God's Christian development of Western Civilization occurred when the Apostle Paul was led of the Holy Spirit to turn west toward Europe instead of east toward Asia during his first missionary journey. The Acts of the Apostles tell us that Paul and Timothy "were forbidden of the Holy Ghost to preach the word in Asia" (Acts 16:6).

Paul had been inclined to go to Bithynia, near the modern-day border of Turkey and Russia, and would have, had it not been for the Holy Spirit directing him west into Greece. It was the Gospel of Jesus Christ, as preached by Paul in the West, that gave western man the individual liberty mentioned by Von Mises and is unknown to orientals.

Solid Ground

We believe Von Mises is on solid ground when he says:

"The sound money principle has two aspects. It is affirmative in approving the market's choice of a commonly used medium of exchange. It is negative in obstructing the government's propensity to meddle with the currency system...

"Sound money means metallic standard. Standard coins should be in fact a definite quantity of the standard metal as precisely determined by the law of the country. Only standard coins should have unlimited legal-tender quality. Token coins and all kinds of moneylike paper should be, on presentation and without delay, redeemed in lawful standard money...

"The great inflations of our age are not acts of God. They are man-made, or to say it bluntly, government-made. They are offshoots of doctrines that ascribe to governments the magic power of creating wealth out of nothing and making people happy by raising 'the national income...'

"Such a policy of radical inflationism is, of course, extremely popular. But its popularity is to a great extent due to a misapprehension of its effects. What people are really asking for is a rise in the prices of those commodities and services they are selling while the prices of those commodities and services which they are buying remain unchanged...

"For the naive mind there is something miraculous in the issuance of *fiat money*. A magic word spoken by the government creates out of nothing a thing which can be exchanged against any merchandise a man would like to get. How pale is the art of sorcerers, witches and conjurers when compared with that of the government's? The government, professors tell us, can raise all the money it needs by printing it...And how malicious and misanthropic are those stubborn supporters of outdated economic orthodoxy who ask governments to balance their budgets by covering all expenditures out of tax revenue!

"These enthusiasts do not see that the working of inflation is conditioned by the ignorance of the public and that inflation ceases to work as soon as the many become aware of its effects upon the monetary unit's purchasing power. When the inevitable consequences of inflation appear and prices soar, they think that commodities are becoming dearer and fail to see that money is getting cheaper."[27]

The U.S. monetary system today is about as far from Von Mises' standards for sound money as you can get. Dr. W. Cleon Skousen, president of The Freeman Institute in Salt Lake City, wrote President Ronald Reagan in 1982 expressing enthusiasm about "Reaganomics" because he believed the principles of it are sound but suggested elimination of the Federal Reserve System and attached a reform plan to base U.S. currency on gold and silver. Its major points include:

• Money is a unit to facilitate the exchange of goods and services, and the right to create money belongs to those who create the goods and services. The Constitution ratified by the people delegated that right to the people's representatives in Congress only and made no provision for Congress to give that right to the group of private bankers who own and control the misnamed Federal Reserve.

• Congress has the never-used responsibility to establish a mechanism for monitoring the money supply so it will remain in balance with the amount of goods and services being produced by the people. To "fix" and maintain the "value" of the dollar as provided in the Constitution, Congress also can prevent money manipulators from draining dollars out of the system to cause depressions or adding artificial dollars to it to create inflation.

• Any paper dollars issued by the government (after elimination of the Federal Reserve) must be redeemable in silver or gold. A large enough supply of the precious metals to redeem lawful money should be stored in government vaults, not speculated with abroad or "cornered" at home by private interests.

• Banks should not be allowed to make loans on non-existent money or "credit." Fractional reserve banking is fraudulent and should be outlawed.

Monetary Freedom

Such reforms would restore authority of Congress to issue the people's money, allow creation of money as needed without borrowing or paying interest for it, get the United States out of debt, balance money with goods and services, stabilize the dollar, curb inflation and depression, reduce taxes and bankruptcies, stabilize prices, increase business and reduce taxes.[28]

Congressman Ron Paul of Texas has introduced a bill he calls "The Monetary Freedom Act" in the 96th, 97th and 98th Congresses to, as he puts it, "restore some stability and freedom to our chaotic and regulated domestic monetary system." He says that the Federal Reserve is increasing the money supply at an annual rate of sixteen to eighteen per cent, far beyond the actual growth rate of the Gross National Product, and that a debt crisis of major proportions threatens to collapse the American and international economies if something is not done soon to stop the Fed's irrational printing of paper money.

Congressman Paul insists that the first order of business for monetary reform is an assay, inventory and audit of the nation's gold reserves—supposedly millions of ounces, but no one knows because there has never been a public report of an assay, inventory and audit. This would be the first provision, "Title I" of Paul's monetary reform bill, to be conducted by the Secretary of the Treasury and double-checked by an independent auditing firm under contract with the General Accounting Office.

Other provisions of Paul's proposed monetary reform bill would require Congressional approval for the sale of gold from the treasury (if there is any gold still there pending assay, inventory and audit); prevent any president from seizing gold as FDR did, an act Congressman Paul calls "a massive theft"; reaffirm the Constitutional rights of citizens to coin, trade, melt, hold, own or use gold in any legitimate manner; repeal federal legal tender laws, which Paul says illegally allowed the government to shift from gold and silver to paper and copper without any legal recourse by the people; redeem all Federal Reserve and U.S. notes in gold.

"I would hope that this Congress could be persuaded to reform our present monetary system before it leads to a devastating financial collapse," Paul says.[29]

Paper Money Pitfall

When the Founding Fathers wrote the Constitution in the summer of 1787, the paper money scandal of late colonial and Revolutionary War times was still fresh on their minds. The Continental Congress had fallen into the same easy and popular policy the Federal Reserve has adopted—issuing paper money in unlimited amount. In addition, several states were issuing their own paper money. The inflated monetary confusion finally brought down the financial house—the Continental Congress's over-issued, and eventually worthless, paper money, giving rise to the popular phrase "not worth a Continental."

The states and the continental government had issued so much money to "pay" for the revolution that the money supply resembled that in the United States today, with a dollar worth 10 percent or less of its face value. Trying to persuade the American people to ratify the Constitution, Alexander Hamilton, James Madison and John Jay wrote a series of newspaper articles which came to be known as "The Federalist Papers." In article, or "paper" No. 44, Madison wrote the following about paper money:

"The loss which America has sustained since the peace, from the pestilent effects of paper money on the necessary confidence between man and man, on the necessary confidence in the public councils, on the industry and morals of the people, and on the character of republican government, constitutes an enormous debt against the States chargeable with this unadvised measure which must long remain unsatisfied, or rather, an accumulation of guilt, which can be expiated no otherwise _____ary sacrifice on the altar of justice of the power which has been the instrument of it."[30]

Madison was saying then what Von Mises said in 1912, what Skousen and Paul and others are saying today. *The issuance of paper money has been abused and must be stopped without explicit approval and orders from Congress, not to states or such private agencies as the Federal Reserve, but to the U.S. Treasury only.* Otherwise, there is no accountability to the people whose work made the money possible.

When currency is not backed by gold or silver, and some of that actually in currency for tangible evidence, the only limits on how much money can be created by government or Federal Reserve or any other authority are prudence and common sense, neither a commodity that governments or bankers or any other money dealers have ever had in abundance.

The reliance upon God, instead of man, by the framers of our Constitution is a necessary basis for a republican form of government and free enterprise, as opposed to tyranny and state socialism. The Founding Fathers trusted God, not man. That's why they divided the power of the Federal government into three parts, checking and balancing one another—the executive (president), legislative (Congress) and judicial

(Supreme Court). They did not trust imperfect, self-centered man and so divided the power of government among three different authorities. "In God We Trust" has been on our coins since the nineteenth century, and whether that is collectively true anymore as a nation, it is, nevertheless, the original basis for the founding of this nation. It was Christians seeking religious freedom, trusting in God and fleeing man-made, government-made tyranny that brought the first permanent and lasting settlers to these shores whose progeny founded the country.

It was man's individual freedom, found through Jesus Christ, that the apostle Paul preached in the Gospel—a freedom (indeed a gospel)unknown in the Orient, from which Paul was turned away by the Holy Spirit. Had Paul been allowed to go east instead of west, would there be a United States of America today, founded in liberty and justice and freedom? Not very likely. America is the pinnacle of Western Civilization, more so than even parliamentary Great Britain or any other country in the West.

It has been individual freedom, just as the economist Von Mises commented, upon which the great economic system of the West has been based—the free enterprise system. Certainly, at times, that freedom has been abused; but through Congress and the courts, through a division of powers instead of a central dictatorship, those abuses have been, and still are being, brought under control, sometimes excessively.

The great corporations of America, comprising the backbone of American business, industry and free enterprise, are owned by millions of stockholders, not just one man. Here again, the division of man's power comes into play, just as it does in American government. The intelligent man, the prudent man with common sense, the God-fearing and God-reverent man will place his trust in God above man, and divide the power of man so man will not be all-powerful and all corrupt. Such division is not tyranny but assures more freedom—free government, free enterprise, free man under God.[31]

The Inflationary Spree

Many people today believe they are "better off" than their parents financially, but, as their income rises, they don't believe their children will fare as well as they do. More Americans are making more "money" today than ever before, or so it seems.[32]

The trouble is that the "money" they are making is not really money but is a substitute for money—fiat money issued on command of the government, paper money with nothing to back it up. They are living on an inflationary spree.

People making more money notice that they also are paying higher prices. As more and more paper money is printed and goes into circulation, prices rise, not because the goods or services are any more valuable, but because the paper money is worth less and less. There is no more wool or cotton in a suit of clothes than there was fifty years ago, but it costs more because the money is cheaper. The $10,000 or $15,000 automobile of today is, in fact, less of a car than an automobile of that same price ten or fifteen or twenty years ago. The automobile itself is not as valuable as its predecessor, but the value of money has depreciated even faster than the value of materials and labor represented in automobiles.

The United States has followed an inflationary monetary policy since the creation of the Federal Reserve; and the policy has been a contributing factor to the nation's worst wars, worst depressions and recessions, and most deceitful times of prosperity in its history. The inherent danger of an inflationary money policy is excess. Once the principle is put into practice, there seems to be no stopping it. The economist Von Mises puts it this way:

"Inflationism is that monetary policy that seeks to increase the quantity of money. Native inflationism demands an increase in the quantity of money without suspecting that this will diminish the purchasing power of the money. It wants more money because, in its eyes, the mere abundance of money is wealth. Fiat money! Let the state 'create' money and make the poor rich, and free them from the bonds of the capitalists! How foolish to forego the opportunity of making everybody rich and consequently happy that the state's right to create money gives it. How wicked of the economists to assert that it is not within the powers of the state to create wealth by means of the printing press!

"The collapse of an inflation policy carried to its extreme—as in the United States in 1781 and in France in 1796—does not destroy the monetary system, but only the credit money or fiat money of the state that has overestimated the effectiveness of its own policy. The collapse emancipates commerce from the state monetary system and establishes metallic money again."[33]

If Von Mises is right—and history seems to sustain his thesis—the United States should not wait for the collapse of the fiat or credit money system that prevails in the economy today but should take steps immediately to reform it and to reinstall metallic money into the currency and the system.

The Case for Gold
President Reagan was aware of this crisis. He appointed a "Gold Commission" to study the possibility of returning to a gold standard, but the commission failed to recommend that. It also failed to obtain an assay, inventory and audit of the U.S. gold supply, if any; and it seemed obvious that the majority of the gold commissioners were either under the influence of the paper and electronic money interests, that is, the bankers, or were simply afraid of the political consequences of instituting monetary reform.

Not so the minority, which issued its own report on the investigation of the Gold Commission and its opening paragraph had this to say:

"More and more people are asking if a gold standard will end the financial crisis in which we find ourselves. The question is not so much IF it will help or IF we will resort to gold but WHEN. All great inflations end with the acceptance of real money—gold—and the rejection of political money—paper. The stage is now set; monetary order is of the utmost importance. Conditions are deteriorating, and the solutions proposed to date have only made things worse. Although the solution is readily available to us, powerful forces whose interests are served by the present system cling tenaciously to a monetary system that no longer has any foundation. The time at which there will be no other choice but to reject the current system entirely is fast approaching. Although that moment is unknown to us, the course that we continue to pursue will undoubtedly hurtle us into a monetary abyss that will mandate a major reform."[34]

Objections to a gold standard monetary system are mostly propaganda put out by those who benefit most from the paper standard—internationalist-minded bankers, who get first crack at the phony money through the deposit multiplier and fractional reserve banking; the government, which is the biggest borrower of paper money from the Federal Reserve; large corporations, also big borrowers; and, oddly enough, welfare recipients and the businesses that live off of them. Welfare recipients and the government-programs designed for them are paid in paper money.

Gold standard critics say there is not enough gold to support the multi-billion dollar national economy. With a gold standard, it would not be a multi-billion dollar paper economy, but an economy just as big, just as vibrant, just as growing—but with a true value figure instead of an inflated paper value figure. As good a way as any to put it is to say that in paper money a suit may cost $400, but in gold it would cost $20, or less. That's the difference in phony paper and real money, and the suit itself has nothing to do with it.

We are talking about a philosophy of money, a theory of money here. For years the predominant and popular money philosophy has been to let government and banks create "money" out of nothing in the manner of John Maynard Keynes. This has led to the inflation that causes high prices, high interest rates, unemployment, destroyed savings, lack of capital for investment, tremendous debts (both public and private)—the entire financial crisis in which we find ourselves.

It is time to try a different philosophy, a philosophy of sound money, before the paper tower held together with chicken wire and chewing gum comes tumbling down around us.

All of our worldly concern about money and monetary systems and such is, in the end, only folly anyway. We came into this world with nothing and will leave it with nothing. But, while we are here, we should take the best financial advice available, which is found in the best book available, the Holy Bible.

The Bible Knows Best

You can buy all the money books and get-rich-quick books and how-to-succeed books you can find in any big bookstore and read them all and you won't get any better advice from any of them than can be found in the Bible. The Bible is God's Word, and He has things to say about money and the stewardship of it, just as He does about life and its conduct. Following is some of the best financial advice from the Bible:

Proverbs 3:5-10: "Trust in the Lord with all thine heart, and lean not unto thine own understanding. In all thy ways acknowledge him and he shall direct thy paths. Be not wise in thine own eyes: fear the Lord and depart from evil. It shall be health to thy navel and marrow to thy bones. *Honor the Lord with thy substance and with the firstfruits of all thine increase.* So shall thy barns be filled with plenty and thy presses shall burst out with new wine."

Luke 6:38: *"Give and it shall be given unto you*; good measure, pressed down, shaken together, and running over, shall men give unto your bosom. For with the same measure that ye mete withal it shall be measured to you again."

Psalm 62:10: "Trust not in oppression and become not vain in robbery: if riches increase, set not your heart upon them."

Matthew 6:19-21: "Lay not up for yourselves treasures upon earth, where moth and rust doth corrupt, and where thieves break through and steal. But lay up for yourselves treasures in heaven, where neither moth nor rust doth corrupt, and where thieves do not break through or steal. *For where your treasure is, there will your heart be also."*

1 Timothy 6:6-12: "But godliness with contentment is great gain. For we brought nothing into this world and it is certain we can carry nothing out. And having food and raiment let us be therewith content. But they that will be rich fall into temptation and a snare, and into many foolish and hurtful lusts, which drown men in destruction and perdition. *For the love of money is the root of all evil*: which while some coveted after, they have erred from the faith, and pierced themselves through with many sorrows. But thou, O man of God, flee these things and follow after righteousness, godliness, faith, love, patience, meekness. Fight the good fight of faith, lay hold on eternal life, whereunto thou art also called and hast professed a good profession before many witnesses."

Philippians 4:11: "For I have learned, in whatsoever state I am, therewith to be content."

3 John 2: "Beloved, I wish above all things that thou mayest prosper and be in health, even as thy soul prospereth."

Proverbs 22:4: "By humility and the fear of the Lord are riches, and honor, and life."

James 1:7: "Every good gift and every perfect gift is from above."

2 Corinthians 9:6: "He which soweth sparingly shall reap also sparingly; and he which soweth bountifully shall reap also bountifully."

Proverbs 6:6: "Go to the ant, thou sluggard; consider her ways, and be wise."

All beneficial books of financial advice and about money matters must coincide with the original advice from the Bible. The verses we have cited are just a few pertaining to health, wealth and wisdom. They do not insist on poverty, but they do warn about the danger of covetousness and greed. They say, like the ant, that you must work for yourself to succeed and not lie about waiting for God or anyone else to give something to you. The Bible advises us that we are mere temporary stewards of whatever goods and possessions God puts in our hands. It tells us that we must honor God with gifts to Him, to His work. It declares that those who give will receive more abundantly than they give; that those who sow much, reap much.

Stewardship Standards

These are all fundamental rules for financial stewardship. The reason most people—and for that matter, most nations—have financial problems is that they don't follow the fundamental rules of financial stewardship set out clearly by the Bible.

As it says in Timothy, love of money is the root of all evil. Notice that it does not say that money itself is the root of all evil but "*love of money.*" God provides us with our needs. He tests our stewardship with money and other possessions His will places in our hands. If we are not good stewards with small amounts, we have no reason to expect Him to trust us with larger amounts. If we do not give, we have no reason to expect to receive. If we do not sow bountifully, we should expect only impoverished reaping. All this is basic Bible finance.

These Biblical facts are not hard to understand. They say that there is no free ride, that you don't get something for nothing and that you can't make something out of nothing.

The government and the banks and the Federal Reserve may have deceived millions of people with paper money and making money out of nothing, but such deception is intrinsically wrong and cannot go on indefinitely. The paper money made out of nothing will, in due time, return to nothing—its true value.

America certainly needs monetary reform, but the way things are in America today, that is impossible with moral reform. The immoral monetary system we have today cannot stand. Only a moral monetary system standing on honesty and the fundamental financial principles set out in the Bible can be of any true value.

In other words, America must turn to God before it turns to money. If America gets right with God, it will get its money right.

Chapter 4

CAPITALISTS AND COMMUNISTS:
THE PERVERTED PARTNERSHIP

Cartel Control

Capitalism has financed the Bolshevik Revolution and nurtured the growth of communism throughout the twentieth Century.[1]

What seems to be a paradox is nothing of the sort. The super-rich cartel control capitalists—represented throughout the ages by the likes of the Rothschilds, Morgans and Rockefellers and, to a lesser extent, by such capitalist comrades of communism as Cyrus Eaton and Armand Hammer—want more than just profitable monopolies; they want monopolistic control of the entire world economy.

What the cartel control capitalists want is the same thing that the communists want—control of a one-world government to rule the world economy.

Why then, if the communists in their Manifesto have vowed to destroy the capitalists, would the capitalists finance communism? There can be only one explanation—so they can CONTROL it. And this is precisely what they are trying to do.

The great land mass of Russia, with its multi-millions of people, has been seen by the cartel control capitalists for years as the world's richest potential market, even more so than China because there is more land with fewer people on it in Russia. This massive land has absorbed and destroyed would-be conquerors from Genghis Khan to Napoleon to Hitler. Military conquest has failed historically, but economic conquest by financial development and control is another matter.

The cartel control capitalists financed Lenin and Trotsky's takeover of Kerensky's government and the Bolshevik Revolution along with it, and since then, have—through Stalin, Khrushchev, Brezhenev and Andropov—financed the industrial growth, military strength and computer-age technological development of Soviet Russia's communist state in order, they think, to control it and to exploit, to turn its alleged "vitality and force" to their own purpose.

BY SADDLING REVOLUTIONARY RUSSIA WITH AN ECONOMIC SYSTEM THAT CANNOT SUCCEED—COMMUNISM—THE CARTEL CONTROL CAPITALISTS BELIEVE THEY CAN CONTROL AND EXPLOIT IT.

They do not reckon that godless communism, a tool of Satan, may be something beyond their power. They recognize the inherent economic weakness of communism, and their covetousness for control of the Russian market blinds them to Satan's unearthly power that is part of communism's ruthless political and military strength.

Whether the cartel control capitalists are mistaken about their plan to control Russia remains to be seen, but no other explanation makes sense or fits the historical evidence. The cartel control capitalists have never been truly interested in American democracy or the republic for which it stands. They have never been interested in other smaller capitalists or any other political or financial or economic systems except for how they might be exploited to help them in their drive to establish and control a *one-world government* that will assure a global economic monopoly.

The Motivation

Whether capitalism or communism succeeds in doing this is a matter of indifference to the power players just so long as they control the winner. It is control—power, not just money—that is the motivation.

It is this explanation that makes sense of Franklin Roosevelt's diplomatic recognition of Soviet Russia in 1933, of excessive Lend-Lease to Russia during World War II, of the "gift" of the U.S. Treasury money plates, of the massive post-war foreign aid to Russia, of the "sweetheart" trade deals, of the wheat deals, of detente and of the technology leakage of the current computer age.

This explanation makes sense of the extensive dealings with the communists by billionaires Cyrus Eaton and Armand Hammer and his father before him—of how they managed to "smuggle" grain and other contraband to the communists before diplomatic recognition was extended by FDR, of how they established mining and manufacturing trusts in Russia, of how these particular on-the-scene capitalists became lifelong communist favorites.[2]

This explanation makes sense of the deal in 1926 between the Rockefellers' Standard Oil of New York and its subsidiary, Vacuum Oil Co., to market Soviet-produced oil in European countries, which included a $75 million loan to the still struggling Bolsheviks.[3]

This explanation makes sense of the strange career of the first U.S. military attache to Moscow—then Colonel, but later, General Phillip R. Faymonville—who spoke Russian, who was a veteran of the American expeditionary force in Siberia that failed to curb communism after World

War I, who became military aide-de-camp and trusted adviser to President Franklin D. Roosevelt. A secret U.S. Army intelligence report on Faymonville says he was more liked and trusted by the Red Army general staff than any other foreign military attache.[4]

This explanation makes sense of the David Rockefeller visit with Khrushchev to promote U.S.-Soviet trade in 1964, the subsequent Rockefeller contacts with President Lyndon B. Johnson, and Johnson's 1966 announcement of "building bridges" to Eastern Europe at a time when communist-bloc weapons and ammunition were being used to kill American servicement in Vietnam.[5]

Scruples Scrapped

The lack of patriotic scruples among the cartel control capitalists and the banks through which they have long owned and controlled the banking industry is evident not only in the financing of godless communism, but in the incredible bankrolling of Hitler's Nazi Germany.

This was engineered by a banker with the oddball name of Dr. Hjalmar Horace Greely Schacht, who was to become Hitler's finance director. Schacht was born in the German province of Schleswig in 1877, shortly after his parents returned from a trip to the United States where Greely, the New York newspaper editor, had colorfully—but unsuccessfully—sought Republican presidential nomination in 1876 only to lose out to Rutherford B. Hayes, the eventual winner over Samuel Tilden in one of the closest and most disputed of American elections.

The Schachts were descendants of German nobles, and their son Hjalmar took a Ph.D. in finance at the University of Hamburg, became a director of the Dresdner Bank at age twenty-six, was financial advisor to General Von Bissing in occupied Belgium during World War I, and in 1922 was appointed president of the Reichsbank, the German central bank, by Chancellor Hans Luther.

It was as head of the Reichsbank that Schacht coldly directed the printing of bales of worthless German paper marks to deliberately bring on the inflation disaster in Germany in the early 1920s. This was part of Schacht's plan to rebuild German finance with other nations' money, as we shall see.[6]

Germany had abandoned gold backing of its currency in 1914 to finance the war by borrowing (meaning issuing paper money) instead of by savings or by politically unpopular taxation—the same manner in which the Vietnam War was financed by the Johnson administration fifty years later. As a result, prices in Germany doubled between 1914 and 1919, just as they did in the United States in just over five years after the Vietnam War.[7]

German bankers, headed by Schacht, and German industrialists made no attempt to curb the inflationary printing of paper money, just as the Federal Reserve and American bankers have declined to do so in current times. The German industrialists—Krupp (arms), Thyssen (steel), Farben (chemicals), Stinnes (manufacturing)—reasoned that cheaper marks would make German goods cheap and easier to export. Export earnings could buy raw materials abroad for both manufacturing and for military stockpiling. Inflation kept everyone working, at least temporarily.

A Wheelbarrow of Money

The paper money presses rolled night and day. Soon, a cup of coffee cost 7,000 marks. It took a wheelbarrow full of marks to buy a loaf of bread. The flight from the virtually worthless currency touched off a buying spree into, first, diamonds, real estate and antiques, then later anything of value down to soap, pins and bric-a-brac. Petty thievery of copper and brass and gasoline from automobiles increased. Prostitution became commonplace. The much-lionized German "cabaret" life of the 1920s boomed as the marks were exchanged for entertainment. Cocaine became fashionable and abundant.[8]

All this suffering and immorality was brought upon the German people by Dr. Schacht and his banking-industrial cohorts as part of the central banker's financial scheme to obtain foreign money of value in exchange for the worthless marks he was debasing as fast as he could by over-printing them. It worked this way:

German marks were purchased by eager speculators, financed largely by bankers and including banks and bankers themselves, in London, Paris, Amsterdam, Switzerland and New York, long after they had become worthless. Bundles could be purchased for a song—for a few pennies. The risk was worth it, it seemed to the speculators, should the mark bounce back. The speculation provided Schacht and the German control capitalists with much-needed foreign exchange at little or no cost except for printing...never mind the suffering of the people and the decline of morality. This unsettled state of financial affairs compelled international bankers to apply the Young Plan in 1924, which relieved Germany of much of its war reparation obligations under the Treaty of Versailles, initiated a new international banking racket in German railroad and industrial bonds, and set in motion the evolution of the Bank for International Settlements.[9]

Hitler's "Angel"

Fritz Thyssen, the so-called "Steel King" of Nazi Germany, was the major benefactor of the Young Plan, which sold bonds to international bankers to finance reconstruction of German railroads and industries in the 1920s. Thyssen received the bulk of the bond receipts so his steel empire could be revived to supply steel for the new railroads and industries, including Krupp's armaments factories. Thyssen was the first of the big German industrialists to contribute funds to Hitler and his Nazi Party, starting as early as 1928—five years before Hitler was to come to power. In this manner, Hitler's money came from the printing presses of the Federal Reserve into the hands of American international bankers, who, with their foreign banking partners, bought German bonds, the receipts of which went largely to Thyssen and then to Hitler and his Nazis.[10]

These illustrations of how unproductive communism and impoverished facism were financed by American and international banks and bankers are to show that big banks and bankers have a responsibility for their actions, whether they believe it or not, and must (or should) suffer the consequences for them when they are wrong. But it doesn't always work that way. As Ogden Nash once said, "Bankers are just like other people, only richer."

The "other people" might be richer, too, if they had going for them what bankers have—the deposit multiplier that makes bookkeeping money out of nothing, and the support of the Federal Reserve that prints infinite amounts of paper money to pay for most banking mistakes.

Other People's Money

Those two schemes (or scams) are the two basic branches of banking: (1) The negotiation of credit through the loan of other people's money and (2) the granting of credit through the issue of notes and bank balances that are not covered by money.

The difference between No. 1 and No. 2 is that No. 1 is, in effect, a cash transaction involving something of value; whereas, No. 2 is a credit transaction, an exchange of present goods for future goods.

These break down into other sophisticated activities of banking, but, in general, No. 1 and No. 2 are what banking is all about.[11]

With the power of money concentrated in their hands, it is bankers who decide who succeeds and who fails in society by making or not making a loan. Among the first to succeed, bankers have decided, are bankers themselves. It was by making insider loans to themselves or to their friends, almost regardless of risk, that bankers established the pattern or habit of making high-risk loans to other interests. This is the philosophical source of the world banking crisis of the 1980s, which was caused by big international bankers making high-risk foolish loans to Third World "less developed countries," or so we are led to believe. It could be part of a massive financial world-control plot to drain the financial power of the industrial world into the abyss of the undeveloped world, making it easier for the bankers of the Bank for International Settlements to control all of the world. Take your pick.

The Thin Line

At any rate, the line between fast-dealing bankers and their insider businessmen friends—and mere criminals—is not always clear. As former Massachusetts Commissioner of Banks Dr. Carol S. Greenwald says,

"What is clear is that what is unfair may not be illegal…if you rob a bank with a gun and you are caught, you definitely go to prison. If you embezzle the bank's funds, you may go to prison. But if you sit on the bank's board as a director and make 'loans' to yourself (or to friends) that are not repaid, you remain a respected businessman in the community even after the regulators punish you by making you resign from the board. Heads you win; tails you don't lose much."[12]

The same apparently goes for making huge international "loans" through the complex international banking chain that transcends mere national boundaries and banking laws. The international banking complex comprising the Bank for International Settlements, the United Nations' International Monetary Fund and World Bank, and the multi-national banks such as Chase Manhattan, with huge branch offices in Moscow and Peking, are simply beyond the power of local or even national regulators or prosecutors to reach.

As economist-author Martin Mayer says, **"With a little ingenuity, a bank president can conceal almost completely from his directors, examiners and auditors loans that he is making for his own benefit."[13]**

That would go for all kinds of loans, including big international ones and high-risk speculation. The record is littered with this kind of wreckage: Billie Sol Estes' bankers, Bert Lance's speculations, the failure of Penn Square in Oklahoma City from over-speculation in oil leases, Continental Illinois of Chicago's underwriting of Penn Square's misadventures, Chase Manhattan's laughable belly-flop into the Drysdale housing bond scam—it goes on and on. These are just a few that came to light in recent times. Heaven only knows how many got away with it. The less scrupulous of the banking fraternity contend they can hardly be blamed for such high-jinks when, after all, the Big Daddy of American banking, the Federal Reserve, sanctions such scams as fractional reserve bnaking, the deposit multiplier and infinite printing of worthless paper money. So what's wrong with loaning a few billion to Mexico in return for the promise of oil production? Why no loan to the communists when they promise a high return of interest? Can't we trust them? Brazil has great potential for development doesn't it? A few billion or so won't hurt. More billions to Zaire make up a virtual mortgage on the entire country! Isn't that worth it?

So big bankers think. And so they have created the international debt crisis of the 1980s. The philosophy is traceable directly to the something-for-nothing policy of the Federal Reserve. It is easy to spend and throw around money that is not your own. Ask Congress. Ask any tyrant.

The Tentacles Tighten

It is as much the fault of bankers as it is politicians that America disregarded George Washington's admonition not to become entangled in foreign alliances. The early colonists came to these shores for religious freedom. They declared independence to be free from taxation without representation by a foreign king and parliament financing other wars of their own making, without regard to those being taxed to pay for them. Millions of American immigrants came into this country for the same reasons for 200 years—to find religious and personal freedom and to escape unfair and burdensome taxation. Today, with trillion dollar national debts and billion dollar annual deficits, some of their descendants may wonder if they came to the right place.

After two world wars—or actually the same war with two divisions with a twenty-year respite for revival of the combatants in between—the United States was a world power and irrevocably entangled with the rest of the world. Enmeshed in the tentacles of the United Nations' Bretton Woods monetary agreement, the International Monetary Fund, the World Bank, the General Assembly, the Security Council, the World Health Organization, the United Nations Education, Social and Cultural Organization (UNESCO), the UN Export-Import Bank, the Bank for International Settlements, the North Atlantic Treaty Organization, the Southeast Asia Treaty Organization and dozens of other international pacts, agreements, technical and cultural ties, to say nothing of world-wide business, American finance became interlocked with international finance. The American taxpayer is the chief financier of the world.

David Rockefeller of Chase Manhattan Bank can't be held solely responsible for this messy state of international financial affairs in which America is now trapped, but he is one—perhaps the leading one—among many bankers of his generation whose thinking and actions along international lines helped create the mess from which we may never extract ourselves.

This is not a treatise about the Rockefellers or David Rockefeller, but certainly the Rockefellers have become the symbolic heirs of the international financier-plotters of one-world government and global economic control begun by the Rothschilds and the House of Morgan and their financial partner-rivals. Rockefellers' founding and financing of the independent Council for Foreign Relations and the Trilateral Commission is well documented in many other works. (See footnote 12, Chapter 1; footnote 9, Chapter 2).

King David

David Rockefeller was more interested in foreign affairs than any of the rest of the family. From the very start of his "career" (which has been spent entirely within the family's Chase Manhattan Bank) he began work in the family bank's foreign department as an assistant manager, lowest of the executive positions, in 1946. That was the year after World War II ended, the year after the formal organization of the United Nations, and the year the U.N. was desperately looking for a permanent home, which the Rockefeller interests conveniently provided by donating property on New York's east side.

By 1948, David Rockefeller was a second vice-president, in charge of Latin America, opening Chase branches in Puerto Rico, Cuba and Panama—the latter two now communist-controlled, while Puerto Rico has a strong communist-backed "independence" movement going. By age forty, in 1955, he was vice-chairman of the board. That was the year Chase absorbed the older Manhattan Bank founded by Alexander Hamilton and Aaron Burr in 1799—Burr later slaying Hamilton in a duel over personal and financial differences. Actually, because of Manhattan's original charter, Manhattan technically took over Chase, but this was merely to get around a legal stumbling block, and the real power was with Rockefeller. At the time of the merger, Chase was the nation's largest bank. Under Rockefeller's international-minded direction, it has dropped to third place in America, largely because nearly seventy-five per cent of its business today is overseas, including major branches involving large real estate developments in downtown Moscow and Peking.[14]

Chase Manhattan is only one superbank controlled by the Rockefellers. National City Bank of New York, the second largest international American bank, was the early beneficiary of William Rockefeller's (John D.'s father) Standard Oil deposits, which made it the largest bank in New York City. James Stillman Rockefeller became "Citibank" president in 1952, while David was still moving up through the Chase heirarchy. Stillman Rockefeller's successor at Citibank was George Moore, whose protege vice-president in charge of the "European District" of the bank was Walter Wriston, who became president in 1967 and chairman in 1969.[15]

Wriston is an internationalist, having specialized in international law and diplomacy at Brown University, where his father was president. He led Citibank full tilt into the interlocked world of American banking and world finance. In the late 1950s and early 1960s, he was the driving force behind Citibank's international expansion from 27 to 61 countries and from 82 to 208 offices worldwide.[16]

A third big New York bank under Rockefeller influence is Chemical Bank, nominally controlled by the Harkness family, which was the largest non-Rockefeller holder of Standard Oil stock until World War II. Edward Harkness was a Rockefeller partner in the old Standard Oil trust.[17]

The Rockefeller banks share interlocked directorships with three of the top insurance companies in America—Metropolitan Life, New York Life and Equitable Life. Through this bank-insurance dynasty, the Rockefellers account for twenty-five per cent of all the assets of the fifty largest banks in America and thirty per cent of all the assets of the fifty largest insurance firms in America. These billions of dollars, controlled through banks and their trust departments and through insurance company

96

assets, establish Rockefeller influence through a major part of the American economy.[18]

If David Rockefeller wants to *play king of the world* by siphoning American finance through the Trilateral Commission and the Council for Foreign Relations by manipulating tax-exempt foundations and directing investments of the International Monetary Fund, he certainly has the financial clout to do it. The international flow of funds eventually must come under the scrutiny of the Bank for International Settlements in Switzerland, and the Rockefellers are the power behind the ex-officio throne that the American Federal Reserve chairman occupies there.

The Strange Catalyst

With the international mind set of David Rockefeller and Walter Wriston and the hundreds of other American bankers they have led and influenced, only the slightest catalyst was needed to touch off a landslide of American money into foreign lands. That catalyst was provided in 1968 when Robert Strange McNamara was named head of the United Nations' World Bank and began the transfer of funds from the western industrial nations into the Third World undeveloped countries, which brought American to the brink of insolvency.

McNamara had headed Ford Motor Company in the 1950s and, as a member of both the Kennedy and Johnson cabinets in the 1960s, was instrumental in plunging America into the Vietnam quagmire. His laughable "electric fence" across the demilitarized zone was supposed to keep the North Vietnamese out of South Vietnam. That was so funny it was tragic. They simply went around it through Laos before tearing it down. It must have been with great relief that Johnson unloaded him on the World Bank in 1968.

For the next thirteen years, McNamara restlessly traveled the world and evolved into the classic internationalist socialist. He was convinced, if enough money was taken from the West in forms of "loans" through the World Bank and the International Monetary Fund and poured into the Third World, that poverty would be no more. He must have inherited that kind of thinking from President Johnson's "War on Poverty" program, which also was a socialist failure.

Under McNamara, the World Bank became less of a bank and more of a development agency for socialist projects everywhere. He tried to reduce the world to statistics and make all of it "bankable." He became an advocate of population control, promoting both birth control and abortion. He became a radical environmentalist. He truly believed the world could somehow spend its way out of poverty. His strident demands for more and more money for the Third World stampeded bankers into following his socialist advice, and the Federal Reserve presses kept rolling off the flood of paper dollars necessary to finance McNamara's transfer of wealth policy.[19]

The Debt Bomb

By 1981 the so-called "debt bomb" was about to go off in the world bankers' face as they realized, too late, that McNamara had been as wrong about transferring wealth to end world poverty as he had been about the electric fence in Vietnam. Banks had over-extended themselves in their loans to Brazil, Mexico, Poland and other communist and Third World countries McNamara had advised them to finance. His resignation from the World Bank was too late to help the bankers he had led into the debt abyss. They needed a bailout and they turned to the International Monetary Fund to get it—and the Fund turned to the U.S. Congress, asking the American taxpayer to underwrite McNamara's folly. Congress balked and world finance teetered on the brink of disaster as the 1980s moved along.

Americans certainly have a stake in international finance, not only as taxpayers but also as individual investors. American savers have entrusted $1.4 trillion to the nation's 15,000 banks. With more than 100 banks having failed in the early 1980s—including Knoxville's United American Bank, the fourth-largest to collapse since the 1930s—Americans have good reason to worry about the safety of their money.[20]

"Banks have done so poorly on so many of their loans that it's embarrassing for them," says Lawrence Ritter, professor of banking at New York University. Ritter says the historical record shows that throughout the 1970s banks lost big money on what at the time seemed like popular investments in oil tankers and then in real estate investment trusts, getting in too late after the real money had been made by others.

"Why didn't the banks foresee these repayment problems?" Ritter pondered. "I question their independence of judgment—they act too much in a herd."

Ritter may be right, considering that the Rothschilds, Morgans, Rockefellers, Federal Reserve, World Bank, International Monetary Fund and Bank for International Settlements have been the herders for centuries. Any bank not in the herd can't tap the money supply.

In the 1980s, as competition for loan interest increased dramatically and domestic investments became scarcer,. banks got wind of loans to "Less Developed Countries," the deadbeats of the Third World that seemed to have "potential" if only they had capital.

The so-called "Third World" is the Third World because it refuses to take sides with the civilized world of Western Civilization and freedom against the barbaric world of communism. The cowards of the Third World try to play it safe, try to play both sides against each other, refuse to make a commitment and generally are more susceptible to Marxist overtures, which promise something for nothing from imagined state assets, than they are to capitalist free enterprise which requires work.

Third World Myths

Let's look at the Third World for a moment, because most of the human race lives there. Poverty is supposed to be its big problem but, in fact, it isn't. The problem is creating wealth. Many geographic regions and social classes of the Third World are not poor at all. Japan, South Korea, Taiwan, Hong Kong, Singapore, Saudi Arabia and Kuwait are hardly suffering. All were poor nations not long ago, but now are comparatively rich nations.

Is the Third World over-populated? Is abortion and birth control the answer to poverty? Not when you consider that if every man, woman and child on earth were relocated into the state of Texas that each person would have 1,700 square feet of living space, or a family of four would have 6,800 square feet, the average size of the American middle-class home including front and back yards. Everyone in the world could move more or less comfortably into Texas and have the rest of the world to develop and live off. Hardly overcrowding or overpopulation. As for concentrations of "teeming masses" in Puerto Rico or Calcutta, Park Avenue has a population concentration that compares with some of the world's worst slums.

Over-population and world food shortage make excellent propaganda devices for the wise and powerful few who would prefer to direct the lives of the foolish many.

Famine, the lack of food or nutrition, is more a political problem than an agricultural one. Too many Third World countries politically prohibit the use of machinery—including tractors and harvesters—on the assumption that machinery reduces jobs. Calls for population control, central planning, and financial control of less educated Third World countries invariably come from politicians and media in the West, controlled themselves by a leadership that wants to wield authoritarian power over the general populace.

The ill-advised bank loans that poured into Third World countries along with "foreign aid" were little more than attempts to buy financial control. The money has been most often used to purchase armaments, to persecute racial and ethnic and political minorities, to cover deficits caused by inefficient and irresponsible government management, and to line the pockets and bank accounts of corrupt officials. [22]

The Tanzania Tragedy

Tanzania in east central Africa has received more "foreign aid" per capita than any nation in the world. Its production per worker has declined fifty per cent in ten years. It has become an importer instead of exporter of corn. Some 150 of 300 private businesses and industries in the nation that were nationalized by the Marxist-dominated government have gone bankrupt due to poor state management. The bureaucracy has grown by fourteen per cent annually, doubling within less than ten years. Dictator

Julius Nyerere, a darling of the liberal international news media as a "black leader", goes unopposed in sham elections, and his political prisoners total thousands. International wealth transfers of millions of dollars from the industrialized free enterprise capitalist nations of Western Civilization have had just the opposite results on Tanzania as were intended by the elite financiers and their payrolled intellectual advisers who poured taxpayer and investor money through the banks into Nyerere's potential black paradise.[23]

The Mexican Mess

Mexico, another Third World country, has been loaned $87 billion, second largest national debt to bankers in the Third World behind Brazil. Mexico's bureaucracy and some of its provinces are headed by the communists who incited the 1968 riot and would-be revolution at the University of Mexico. Their revolution failed, but they moved right on into government positions and now control the country. The big debt has prompted Mexico to implement a severe austerity program that has caused its worst recession. The austerity program was begun in 1982 when Mexico nearly defaulted on its debt, and the banks which had loaned the money were saved only by U.S. government emergency funds pumped into Mexico. The austerity program includes tax increases, a clampdown on wages and public spending, curbs on imports and steep devaluations of the peso. This is the fate facing all debtor nations, eventually, including the United States. Mexico is only a preview.[24]

The "emergency fund" that saved Mexico was in dollars from U.S. taxpayers funneled by the American government through the International Monetary Fund. Despite the austerity measures, the only thing the emergency fund did was allow Mexico to repay some even more interest coming due. Like the rest of the Third World countries that have sponged up free world capital, Mexico is not reducing the size of its debt but merely planning to refinance it, a "rollover" as it is popularly known— extend the repayment time indefinitely, reduce the interest payments as much as possible, stall for time, and dictate some cosmetic austerity measures to fool Western bankers into thinking something constructive is being done.

Adios, Argentina

Argentina is yet another Third World country in serious financial trouble with a foreign debt of $43 billion. Argentina alone has enough uncultivated land to feed the entire world population. It has enough beef production to export hundreds of thousands of tons annually. It is self-sufficient in petroleum and natural gas and has some of the richest soil on the globe. But Argentina is a debtor nation instead of a rich country because it has been mismanaged and corrupted politically.

Argentina changed political governments in late 1983, but no on can account for the $43 billion that the former military government borrowed from international bankers. The new government doesn't want to pay a debt it believes was fraudulent in its concept and corrupt in its distribution, but the new government also can't afford to become an international deadbeat because it needs to borrow even more money.

The $43 billion was borrowed without the consent of the people of Argentina by an unelected government that had taken power by force and led the country into the disastrous Falklands Islands fiasco. The international bankers loaned the money because the former government had set unrealistically high interest rates in order to get it, rates averaging 200 per cent per year considering the exchange of dollars for Argentine pesos. The peso was overvalued, and more dollars were borrowed to prevent a devaluation and to assure the bankers of their interest rates.

Dr. Walter Beveraggi Allende, an attorney involved in renegotiation of the Argentine debt, says his investigation of it indicates most of the money went straight back to the bankers who engaged in financial speculation in the dollar-peso exchange, along with high-ranking members of the government. The $43 billion was not invested in capital venture, but, in fact, halted the normal development of industrial, commercial and agricultural business in Argentina and brought the country to the brink of ruin. Only the bankers and what corrupt officials may have escaped the country profited. The people suffer.[25]

Why We Suffer

And the people of the United States suffer along with them as they supply the money at a losing rate of interest to the International Monetary Fund of the United Nations. Here is why:

When the U.S. contributes to the IMF, it receives dormant assets denominated in so-called "Special Drawing Rights" or SDRs in exchange. These SDRs cannot be withdrawn by the United States to pay our own bills here at home, so we have to finance these lost dollars by borrowing on the credit market. This increases our budget deficit, and there is a net loss to the U.S. Treasury because the interest paid out on the credit market is larger than that received from the IMF on the U.S. reserve account.

It means we lose a little more money each time we contribute to the IMF because Treasury notes sell at about eight per cent, and the return on U.S. reserves (contributions) to the IMF is seven per cent. In 1982 that net loss amounted to $1.3 billion.

It is, as one U.S. Senator calls it, a vicious circle. Senator John Melcher of Montana, debating against an additional $8.5 billion in U.S. funds for the IMF said, "It is rather odd that we are going to borrow money on behalf of the U.S. taxpayers in this generation and the generations to come on which we are going to continually pay interest, to up our contributions to the International Monetary Fund so they, in turn, can provide it to countries so they can shovel it through their governments to pay interest on some bad debts owed to banks. (As is the case in Argentina, the senator might have added.) This is a circle, all right, and it is a very vicious circle.

"We should not take taxpayers dollars for that purpose. We should not, by all that is holy—there ought to be something holy reserved in our principles—we should not borrow money to turn over to the International Monetary Fund so that banks with bad loans can have their interest, mind you, on bad foreign loans, paid to them."[26]

The Big Red Loan

The bad loans to Mexico, Argentina, Brazil, the communists of Eastern Europe and the Marxists of Africa were just warm-up loans compared with the BIG LOAN being designed for Red China. This is the one that could finally break America.

After the 1984 election, regardless of who wins it, there will be a tremendous increase in taxation and inflation to finance the big loan to Red China. The groundwork already is being prepared by the international bankers of the IMF, with the approval of the Bank for International Settlements. David Rockefeller's Chase Manhattan Bank didn't build branch banks and office complexes in downtown Moscow and Peking without a master plan for using them. It is found in a Rockefeller's Trilateral Commission report published in 1982 which says:

"Developing countries should have full access to financial markets of the developed countries...the ability of developing countries to meet these challenges (of loan repayments) depends substantially on our willingness to help developing countries meet mounting debt service burdens (through increased support for the IMF and World Bank) and our willingness to engage in other forms of assistance."[27]

The real purpose of the International Monetary Fund World Bank bailout was revealed by World Bank President A.W. Clausen when he demanded a new $20 billion increase in funding for the World Bank in the wake of contributions from member countries led by the U.S. that already was doubling the bank's capital to an estimated $90 billion. Claussen said the money will be needed by 1986 because that's when Red China is scheduled to become a World Bank member and eligible for development loans.[28]

Claussen's plan, or actually that of the international banking fraternity, calls for a massive transfer of American industry and technology to Red China to take advantage of what amounts to Chinese slave labor in that communist country of one billion population.

This planned destruction of American industry will see the establishment of thousands of new factories throughout Red China to exploit the cheap labor. Free workers in America simply cannot be price competitive with goods manufactured by communist slave labor at little or no wages in Red China. The New York Times has already reported "an increased flow of semi-conductor technology, computers and other high-technology products to China."[29]

Secretary of Defense Caspar Weinberger commented at the time that he was "fearful that the technology might be used for military purposes," meaning the development, production, installation and aiming of nuclear weapons and missiles at the United States.[30]

"About fifty American companies in the semi-conductor industry want to sell expertise that the Chinese would use to develop their own capability to produce semi conductors," The New York Times reported. Such Red Chinese industry would be in direct competition with semi-conductors now being produced by American workers.

Red China is also being considered for membership in the Asian Development Bank, supported chiefly by the United States and Japan, which would require "either the expulsion of Nationalist China or relegating it to a subordinate status."[31]

The Terrible Tax

To raise the money in America for "investment" in Red China, a plan was afoot in Congress and in Washington economic circles to institute a new confiscatory taxation scheme shortly after the 1984 election known as a *"consumption tax."* A consumption tax would work this way: any money you invested in government-approved projects (meaning those for the benefit of international bankers, such as the Red China development scheme) would be tax-deductible but the remainder of your money, your total consumption, would be taxed. Any money you borrowed to finance consumption, including home mortgage money, would also be taxed.

This would allow the big investors in Red China and other communist and Marxist and Third World countries to avoid taxation because of their "government approved" investments, but would place a new and crushing tax burden on America's productive middle and working class. The National Bureau of Economic Research reported that a consumption tax would increase Federal tax revenue and bank holdings by $1.4 trillion.[32]

You would think that common sense and prudence on the part of international bankers and financiers would cause them to search for some kind of banking reforms to pull the world back from the brink of bankruptcy. But the crazy thing is that they are doing just the opposite! Instead of curtailing wild and unpredictable loans, they are extending more of them and still planning the biggest yet to Red China.

International bankers and their economists are saying that the most crucial problem of the 1980s is not to rein in the banks but to keep them lending so that the liquidity problems of the big Latin American borrowers do not deteriorate into a vicious circle of economic dislocation. They contend that if the Latin deadbeats can't borrow yet even more money, their demand for goods from industrialized nations will dry up and reverse the fragile American-European economic recovery of the early '80s into a full-blown worldwide depression.[33]

Equitable Economics

Bankers have about the shortest sight of any known myopics on record. They constantly seek first aid remedies for what amount to brain surgery problems. They habitually violate what is perhaps the one basic principle of economics, which has been reduced to one sentence by Henry Hazlitt, the man journalist H.L. Mencken once described as the only economist in history who could really write. Hazlitt's one-sentence principle of economics states:

"The art of ecnomics consists in looking not merely at the immediate but at the longer effects of any act or policy; it consists in tracing the consequences of that policy not merely for one group but for all groups."[34]

Hazlitt is one of the few economists and perhaps the only one who says there is no time left for economic remedies, that the paying time for past mistakes is already here. He says it this way:

"There are men regarded today as brilliant economists who deprecate saving and recommend squandering on a national scale as the way of ecnomic salvation; and when anyone points to what the consequences of these policies will be in the long run, they reply flippantly, as might the prodigal son of a warning father: 'In the long run we are all dead.' And such shallow wisecracks pass as devastating epigrams and the ripest wisdom.

"But the tragedy is that, on the contrary, we are already suffering the long-run consequences of the policies of the remote or recent past. Today is already the tomorrow which the bad economist of yesterday urged us to ignore. The long-run consequences of some economic policies may become evident in a few months. Others may not become evident for decades. But in every case these long-run consequences are contained in the policy as surely as the hen was in the egg, the flower in the seed."[35]

Why should Americans be forced to provide their hard-earned money for "loans" which are actually gifts to deadbeat Latin Americans and every stripe of Marxists and communists? If the government is doing this, then the government is biased in favor not just of big American bankers, but of big international bankers. More frightening, the evidence gives the appearance of the international bankers controlling the government, or, at least, the Federal Reserve which dictates to the Treasury, which in turn collects taxes.

If we don't have to give those tax dollars to Latin and communist deadbeats and thieves, we would get to spend them ourselves as we

see fit. **Why don't we get a choice? When do we get a choice? Will we ever get a choice?**

Until those questions are answered, our money is not safe.

See Both Sides

Look at it this way, through Hazlitt's wisdom of considering long-range consequences: Will the world economy collapse if we don't bail out the bankers and their bad loans? What happens if we don't? One thing for certain is that each of us would have more money individually because it would not be taken for taxes to be sent off to deadbeats through the hands of bankers who would take their cut.

Another thing for certain is that the money then would be spent first in America instead of overseas. That in itself would stimulate the economy as much as waiting for the money to come back from overseas to purchase American goods for Latin and communist customers...and that might not happen at all, and if it did the total would be less than was sent originally.

What we are saying is that the bankers and the politicians who champion them with misleading statements and the media who circulate their propaganda are wrong. If they are right, how did they get in such trouble in the first place? If they are so smart and have such certain solutions, why do they keep having to tap the American taxpayer to bail them out of trouble? Why should we trust foolish big bankers who have made billions of dollars worth of bad loans already with billion, more?

Let them take their loss now. It won't hurt us as much now as it will later, and it certainly won't cost as much now as it will later, after even more billions are foolishly loaned and lost.

Every dollar spent to prop up bad loans is a dollar than cannot be spent for something else in the American economy. The bankers and their political and media friends are not looking beyond the ends of their noses. They are painting us a picture of what they believe will be, first, a banking collapse and second, an economic collapse, if Mexico and the rest of the deadbeats and commmunists the bankers love so much default.

What they are not telling us is what happens to the dollars we keep ourselves and spend in our economy here at home. If those dollars will keep the banking and world economic systems from collapsing, surely they must be powerful enough to keep our American economy afloat and to finance banks that have not made foolish overseas loans. Let's simply spend those dollars at home instead of overseas. Let's cut out the middle men—the government tax collector and the international banker—and pass the dollar on directly from American wage earner-consumer to American producer. If that dollar is beneficial to Mexico or Rumania, won't it be just as beneficial to the United States if spent directly here instead of being routed overseas through the hands of government bureaucrats and big international bankers? Yes, it will be just as beneficial and, in fact, more so because there won't be the two big middle men taking their cut.

The False Focus

How many times have we bought the same old phony argument the bankers and the government and the media are making now? It goes like this:

A big government spending project will create jobs, put money in circulation and provide a permanent improvement such as a dam or bridge or highway or housing for the poor. So the money is taken from you and me and used to hire construction workers and buy materials, and when it is finished, we can see the project before our eyes.

That scenario is sold to us again and again. Certainly, many government projects are worthwhile and there is both a need and a demand for them. But many government projects are promoted merely on the basis of socialist redistribution of wealth without any particular need or demand other than political decision.

What we are saying is that if the money is NOT spent on the government project, it will be spent on something else. It will create jobs in another sector. It will put money in circulation somewhere else, not just where the government dictates it to circulate. It will provide or support a permanent improvement such as the factory built to supply whatever goods the money purchased. It will be used to pay the workers there as surely as it would have been used to pay the workers on the government project.

We don't always see in a single project the benefits of dollars spent on something other than government projects, but the benefits are very real to those receiving them, nevertheless.

This is the case we are trying to make for spending our dollars ourselves intstead of surrendering so many of them through taxation to the government to bail out foolish bankers—or auto manufacturers or city governments or aircraft makers or any other government-favored special interests.

Had we not bailed out Chrysler and New York City and Lockheed and now the bankers and their Latin-communist friends; that same money would have spent in the free market place for the benefit or profit of someone else who was not such a poor manager as to have needed a bailout. Such bailouts mean taking money from the efficient and loaning it to the inefficient. The risk is so high that prudent private enterprise won't take it, so foolish government takes it instead.

Chapter 5

YOU CAN BANK ON THIS

Mad Money

W e are in a new age of banking, with a new kind of money. The new banking created the new money, the electronic and plastic money. The Federal Reserve creates new money, and the new banking system expands it. There is more than $1.4 trillion worth of it floating around today, none of it backed by gold or silver or anything but government order, the "fiat" money.

And there are billions more in new money—that loaned abroad, that listed on bank credit cards, that in equipment such as computers and jet planes owned by banks and loaned to customers for a fee. Billions and billions and billions of dollars the banks made with mirrors through the deposit multiplier by expanding on the paper money printed by the Federal Reserve.

This mad financial activity has caused some new money rules to be drawn up by the bankers, in the form of government legislation. The new rules are being phased in over a period of years, but they are found in a law passed by Congress called the Depository Institutions Deregulation and Monetary Control Act of 1980. **The main feature of this act is that it extends the power of the Federal Reserve over just about every dealer in money.**

Banks simply aren't what they used to be. Having been one of the most highly-regulated businesses, banks also became one of the most law-evading businesses, finding every possible loophole to dodge through in order to avoid regulation. Since 1968, when Citibank of New York created a holding company for itself, most big banks have become holding companies. A holding company can own one or more banks that do traditional banking plus owning several other businesses that have some link to banking such as consumer lending firms (savings and loans and credit unions), insurance companies, equipment leasing, data processing, and travel services that issue money orders and credit cards and other interests. Through these businesses, the bank, through its holding company, can operate across state lines, which is prohibited by law in the United States. A small loan company owned by a bank holding company can operate in many states. So can a commercial finance company. Citicorp, the Citibank holding company, operates in more than forty states.[1]

Another thing the Monetary Control Act of 1980 did was eliminate the interest rate ceilings on what various institutions could pay for deposits. That had been established by the notorious "Regulation Q" of the Federal Reserve. In return for rescinding Regulation Q, the Fed obtained control over nearly all lending institutions.

The Act requires that all banks and other financial institutions which have checkable deposits must hold reserves for those deposits at the Federal Reserve Bank in their district. This not only stopped independent-minded banks from leaving or declining Federal Reserve membership, it extended Fed control to those institutions such as savings and loans and credit unions, which wanted to pay even higher interest to depositors in order to charge yet higher interest to borrowers. It was a political swapout—higher interest and the elimination of Regulation Q for Fed control, largely through the fractional reserve requirement which allows the Fed to regulate the money supply.

In addition, S & Ls and credit unions, known as "the thrifts," are permitted to offer checkable deposits and to make new kinds of commercial and consumer loans. These are business functions which used to belong exclusively to commercial banks. The provisions of the Act are being phased in during the early and mid-1980s.

The competitiveness brought about by these changes will significantly alter the entire structure of what might be called "the financial services industry" in this country. It changes the structure and operation of banking. Small savers should get a bit more interest for their savings, as the banks, S & Ls, and credit unions compete for small saver deposits. And borrowers will pay more, as the Act built-in higher interest rates under the disguise of "time value" of the funds which are borrowed.[2]

The so-called "time value" simply means that the American currency, basically the paper money, is worth less every day; so higher interest rates are designed by the Act to cover the loss of paper money value in the future.

United Nation "Credit"

Knowing that, they loaned infinitely and indiscriminately to nearly all comers throughout the world. The United Nations, through its International Monetary Fund and Word Bank, was glad to give practically all its members a good credit rating, if that's all it took, to transfer billions in wealth from the West and its hard-working industrialized nations to the rest of the world.

Americans won't realize they have been duped into permanently higher interest rates and much lower currency value until the mid-1980s, and later, when the full effects of the Act are phased in.

A Sneaky Angle

There is another sneaky angle to the Act that the news media mostly overlooked. It diminishes the consumer protection provisions of the 1968 Truth-in-Lending Act by placing new limitations on examiners and regulators. Originally, violators of Truth-in-Lending had to reimburse the wronged customers. The new "banking reform" act of 1980 amended the restitution provisions of Truth-in-Lending so that enforcement applies only when creditors inaccurately disclose annual percentage rates or finance charges, and only where the errors resulted from a clear and consistent pattern of violations, gross negligence, or willfulness.

"These are almost impossible standards for a regulator to prove," says Dr. Carol S. Greenwald, the former Massachusetts Commissioner of Banks. "It makes it most unlikely that the bank regulatory agencies will now be able to require any reimbursements for violation."[3]

This put the banks and other financial institutions, now nearly all tools of the Federal Reserve, back into the business of cheating their customers whenever they can get away with it, by arguing that their cheating was not a consistent pattern or gross negligence or willfulness or inaccurate disclosure. To argue those points successfully, the financial institutions' lawyers and bookkeepers will be paid more, while customers, depositors, and savers will be paid less.

A Large Loophole

Another tricky provision of the Act that sounds good, but remains to be proven good, provides that the Fed publish—on a demonstration basis in selected metropolitan areas—the amount of interest rates charged by creditors for consumer credit. The catch is whether the Fed will publish this information by the names of specific lenders, at least monthly, or whether it will merely give a nod to the law and publish area averages on a quarterly basis. The former, if published accurately, would give savers a great guide to the best investments, meaning the banks and the Fed would have to part with more money to prudent Americans who save. The latter would be meaningless to the individual saver. You can see that the loophole here is big enough to drive a Federal Reserve armored car through without being touched by any side of the law.

The Monetary Control Act also destroys the last remnants of what might be called states rights banking. It used to be, from passage of the National Banking Act of 1864 to the Monetary Act of 1980, that a "dual banking system" existed in America, with both state and federal banks.

The introduction of the Federal Deposit Insurance Corporation in 1934 reduced some of the states' authority in granting charters to new banks but didn't eliminate the dual system. The Monetary Control Act brings all banks, whether formally Fed members or not, under control of the Fed's reserve requirements. State banking systems no longer can offer a cheaper alternative of borrowing, or a more profitable one of loaning, for individuals than the federal system. This will inevitably bring state and local political pressure on state banking regulators to be more lax than ever in their enforcement, in order to allow state banks to compete for business with the federal system. In time, all state banks may well decide to join the federal system since they are within the reserve requirement, anyway. Without coming in to the open and saying so, that is an obvious intent of the Monetary Control Act.

The Monetary Control Act also has touched off skirmishing among bank regulators working under different authorities. The FDIC regulators contend they have the right to examine almost any bank in the United States, but they have run afoul of bank officials who claim that only the Office of the Comptroller of the Currency, or else the Federal Reserve Board itself, has authority to examine and regulate their bank.

This appears to be another symptom of the Federal Reserve tightening its grip on all banks—and all money.

Rivalry or Responsibility?

Bank examining, chartering, regulating and disciplining has, for decades, been divided among three agencies. The FDIC examines state-chartered banks that are not part of the Fed system; but, since the Monetary Control Act, those banks consider themselves part of the reserve requirement system and, consequently, part of the Fed system. The Federal Reserve has, for years, supervised state-chartered banks that chose to join the Federal Reserve System. The Comptroller of the Currency supervised nationally-chartered banks.

The traditional financial thinking has been that, if an FDIC-supervised bank fails, the danger to the total banking system and to FDIC's $14 billion insurance fund is minimal. But, if a big bank under supervision of the Fed or the Comptroller shuts down, the threat to not only the banking system, but to the interlocking international banking system and the FDIC insurance fund, would be considerable.

The spat among regulators has been going on for years behind the scenes but burst into public view in 1982 with the failure of Penn Square in Oklahoma City. The FDIC, in the press and in Congressional hearings, said the financial catastrophe could have been smoothed out more equitably if only the Comptroller had informed FDIC of Penn Square's terrible condition sooner than it did. The Comptroller got "revenge" when Knoxville's United American Bank, under FDIC supervision, went belly-up in February of 1983. The solemn pronouncements of the

Comptroller's office hardly concealed the snickering.[4]

This disarray, rivalry, back-biting and manuevering for control cannot be reassuring to individual savers and investors. It makes it appear to a public with little enough knowledge about banking and bank regulation that bureaucratic squabbling for power and control over money is more important than the safekeeping of the American public's money.

The financial powers know that they are going to be all right because they are backed up by the Federal Reserve-controlled money printing presses of the U.S. Treasury Department. The individual investor and saver has no money printing press behind him. When a financial institution fails, only the "suckers" get hurt—the savers and depositors without a printing press behind them and the taxpayers, who get sent the bill for federal "insurance" of deposits in the form of yet another U.S. Treasury Bond printed up and given to the Federal Reserve as an order to print just that much more paper money at taxpayer expense.

The taxpayer must eventually make good on that bill in the form of a bond, either in this generation or the next, or the next, or however many generations have been put in hock by unlimited government spending financed by worthless paper bonds given to the Federal Reserve in return for worthless paper currency. We don't "owe it to ourselves," we owe it to the privately-owned and privately-controlled Federal Reserve, namely, the big international banks and financial interests.

And it is not just "bank failures", or the deposit multiplier, or the fractional reserve requirement banking system that has been placed on the backs of American taxpayers. The taxpayers, collectively known as "Uncle Sucker" to the financial insiders who reap the benefits, also will eventually be responsible for the multi-billion dollars of bad debts owed by communist and Third World nations, loaned money by careless and irresponsible international bankers. Those bankers are safe so long as American taxpayers continue to believe in the value of paper money printed by the U.S. Treasury presses upon order of the Federal Reserve.

These billions or trillions, if any one authority has a complete record, have created an international financial crisis now known popularly as "The Debt Bomb." It would have exploded already but for continual replacement of the burning fuse with an ever more expensive and longer one replaced by the IMF and the World Bank, both financed largely, not by their parent United Nations, but by the United States.

U.S. banks have the largest world commitments, and at least three-fourths of all international loans are made in dollars. This makes the U.S., meaning the U.S. taxpayer, the *world debt underwriter* when it comes to saving the banking world's financial system. It would have to be done through the Federal Reserve drawing upon the U.S. Treasury paper money printing presses. Nations already holding such paper dollars, whether loaned to them or earned by foreign trade, have "special drawing

111

rights" through the International Monetary Fund on the U.S. Treasury through the Federal Reserve. This means the Federal Reserve would have to pump in the dollars that a troubled U.S. creditor bank needed to survive, even if it meant runaway inflation in the U.S.

Bruce Brittain of Salomon Brothers, which is affiliated intricately with the financial interests that control the Federal Reserve, says:

"The international debt crisis can be boiled down to a problem of four countries, ten U.S. banks, and the Federal Reserve."[5]

As inflation gets out of hand as a result of Federal Reserve action— the even more massive printing of paper money—everyone, every taxpayer, is paying a share. As one government official said, "It is a tax to save the system."[6]

Such statements amount to propaganda, already presuming that "the system" is worth saving and that it is incumbent upon the American taxpayer to save it. The financiers and the media they control try to make the crisis appear as an accomplished fact, and failure to resolve it in favor of the bankers would bring about world catastrophe. What they are really afraid of is that it would bring about a banking catastrophe, pulling down the houses made of worthless paper money. Whether that would result in a world financial catastrophe should be debated, not accepted as fact.

The ruin of dishonest money would more likely bring about the ruin of the dishonest than of the entire world or even the inflated American currency system. Is there no room for argument by those who contend a return to a gold standard may be painful but not catastrophic, that the readjustment of the economy to a gold standard would only hurt for a little while and not cause the entire system to fail, as the paper money champions are now claiming?

We are talking about correcting this bankrupt system through fundamental change instead of merely patching temporary bandages on it here and there to keep it going for awhile longer. People are concerned about whether fundamental change would adversely affect their business and their savings. They are understandably afraid that such change might hurt them financially. Such an attitude is somewhat like the sick patient who refuses corrective surgery for an abdominal pain hoping that it will go away or that it can be treated with aspirin. When his appendix finally bursts or cancer kills him six months later, it is too late for surgery, too late for fundamental change in his physiology. The sickness has killed him.

This is what is happening to America financially. We have consumed too much paper money and now we are sick, like a kid in a candy store who ate too much that was not nutritionally good for him. To believe that there is not a day of reckoning, a day of justice, a day of judgment, is to delude oneself. To believe that the patchwork tower of financial instability we have built out of paper money pasted to chickenwire with chewing gum will last eternally and not topple, is to go against every principle of construction, physics and mathematics, to say nothing of honesty.

The American Economy

Let's look at some important segments of the American economy and see what a fundamental change, a transition to a gold instead of paper standard, would do to them:

REAL ESTATE—Real estate, the purchase of residences, is the biggest investment most Americans make because it meets both a need (everyone needs someplace to live) and serves as a hedge against inflation and taxation. In moving to a gold standard, the phony paper money values now attached to real estate would decrease, with prices reverting to an honest level, lowering the now frantic inflationary expectations which place $1 million or $400,000 or $100,000 price tags on what are actually far more modest homes and, as a result, lower taxes on real estate considerably. With lower prices, capital tied up in real estate for protection from inflation and taxation could be shifted into more productive sectors of the economy and bring even greater returns in investment.

Real estate appears to "appreciate" only because paper dollars become worth less as more of them are printed, thus requiring more and more paper dollars to buy the same property. Real estate "booms" are not honestly based on scarcity of land in certain locations, but on inflation. The Florida and Atlantic City real estate booms of the 1920s are examples of how "booming" real estate is liable to go bust because of inflation.

Lower real estate prices would allow more young people, who cannot afford houses at today's inflated paper money prices, to buy homes of their own, creating a new real estate market. More houses would be bought and sold at lower prices in a gold transition. This would expand the property base and give relief to homeowners paying inflated taxes— the very thing which prompted Proposition 13 in California.

Lower taxes would mean less revenue for government, even with an expanded tax base. Less government would mean less bureaucratic and regulatory control of our lives. It would mean less money going into an unproductive segment of the economy—government—and more into business and industrial development, including new and small businesses which have a difficult time starting and remaining in business, with inflated paper money. The large number of bankruptcies in the late 1970s and early 1980s attest to this.

Lower taxes and lower prices would mean lower interest rates on borrowed money. The inflation premium in interest rates would vanish. It would no longer be necessary to charge to the borrower, in interest rates, the lost value of paper money twelve or twenty-four or thirty-six months in the future. Future economic planning and stability would be more certain.

This kind of foresight is the basis for what is called "classic economics." It looks at not only the immediate effects of an economic action, but the long range and "unseen" effects as well. The trendy economist of today likes to talk about immediate satisfaction or gratification of certain interest groups who might benefit from short-sighted economic actions, usually related to government spending. Transition to a gold standard requires more far-sighted economic planning, based on an honest dollar extending far into the future, instead of on sudden injections of dishonest paper dollars for short-term and immediate benefits which have political popularity but are economically disatrous in the long run.

AGRICULTURE—Prices for farm land have risen with inflationary and speculative prices of real estate. Going to a gold standard would decrease the demand for land as an inflationary hedge. Farm commodity prices would decrease but so would wholesale prices on all goods farmers need. The return to a gold standard in 1880 increased the number of farms, farm acreage, farm productivity, and the value of farm output. In other words, real income, not inflationary income, would increase.

SMALL BUSINESS—The end of paper money inflation would cause capital to shift from speculative investments, designed to protect money from inflation and excessive taxation, to productive investments that would benefit the economy. This would cause a beneficial increase in small business because not so much capital would be absorbed by big government and corporate investment for tax avoidance instead of production. Growth in small business would create new jobs, paid for by money not paid into such high taxes and not loopholed for tax avoidance, but spent productively.

HEAVY INDUSTRY—Low, long-term interest rates, resulting from sound money instead of high, short-term interest rates that accompany paper money inflation, would allow much bigger investments in heavy industry, such as steel, automobiles, mining, rubber, railroads, money that now is going into tax shelters of the financial industry, and into government through taxation. The new industrialization of America cannot be done with phony paper money, high taxes, and excessive regulatory control of big government, which have hindered capital investment and long-term planning. Only sound, honest money can make for sound, honest rebuilding of American industry to compete on a worldwide basis with those countries that have used our free paper money to their advantage while we taxpayers paid for it. That money sent overseas as "aid" was tax money that should have been used instead as capital investment in America.

EXPORTS—By investing in American business and industry, instead of in so much taxation that winds up in the hands of foreigners after having passed through big international banking interests, American products would once again have price stability. They could compete internationally. Capital for their production would not be robbed by excessive taxation which has been misspent by government policy. Our balance of trade would become equitable and perhaps even favorable once again after years of losing to the rest of the world. We would stop exporting our own paper money brand of inflation so that each country would not have to move toward protectionism and isolationism, increasing world tensions; and international markets could open for further trade and true investment based on sound money instead of phony, inflationary paper.

BANKING—This is the most critical area of true monetary reform. A gold standard would, among other things, make the Federal Reserve unnecessary. It would put an end to the bank and financial cartel that has ruled America since the Federal Reserve Act of 1913 and the McFadden and Glass-Steagall Acts of the 1930s, which have protected vested banking interests from competition and established their financial control by means of the Fed reserve requirements and the deposit multiplier. Gold standard free banking would allow true banking and financial competition never really known in this country. Free enterprise banking could be entered into by anyone filing necessary legal papers with proper authorities at whatever level of government—local, state, federal—and issuing 100 per cent redeemable notes in gold. As it is, the present banking cartel is about to go bankrupt anyway, according to their own "crisis" and "debt bomb" statements. Their plan is for the taxpayer to bail them out at a cost of billions. A sound money system would relieve existing banks of the inflationary pressures on them and open up the financial business to the kind of competition it should have had all along. The choices of individual investors and depositors in the free market would control the banks instead of the vested financial interests of the Federal Reserve and its government-imposed regulations, both of which have led to the current "banking crisis."

Suckers Pay

The major objections to sound monetary reform come from those who have vested interests in continuing the unsound inflationary paper money system, especially if they are convinced that the U.S. taxpayers eventually will pay for their mistakes. The U.S. taxpayers are the ones who should be insisting upon sound monetary reform and rebelling against paying ever more money, now and in future generations, for a bankrupt monetary system that has enriched a few at the expense of many.

Senator Ron Paul and his colleague Lewis Lehrman put it this way in the conclusion of their minority report by the U.S. Gold Commission:

"It is clear (that a sound monetary reform based on gold) will bring about stable prices and falling interest rates and will open all sectors of the economy to newcomers: new farmers, new homeowners, new small businessmen and new bankers. Those companies that have been subsidized by the government will suffer most from a movement toward freedom. Those who have profited from the misdirection of capital investment by the government will also suffer.

"A 'gold standard recession' however, would be quite different from a paper money recession, such as we are now suffering. Were the government to refuse to interfere with the adjustment process, the recession would be over very rapidly, as we saw in the last 'free market recession' of 1921. And while the recession would be short, it would not be sharp. There would undoubtedly be a tremendous outpouring of new savings and investments in response to the new confidence in honest money and the realization that inflation was a thing of the past. The transition to a gold system will bring increasing prosperity, real growth, lower unemployment, higher real wages, and greater capital investment. The transition to freedom, in short, is the only way out of the economic crisis we are now in."[7]

Conclusion

What To Do Until Sound Money Arrives

There is another alternative to saving the Federal Reserve and its big international banking owners from disaster, but its not the kind of thing they want publicized. It is monetary reform of an entirely different and far more radical kind than establishment of a gold standard. It is a new monetary system altogether based on an entirely new kind of money.

Just for discussion's sake, let's consider this scenario:

One Friday, a payday, everyone gets paid and puts his paycheck in the bank, except for what small change might be needed, and goes home for the weekend. On a Sunday evening, the government announces a plan that has long been secretly in the formulative stage—an entirely new money system will be introduced soon; meanwhile, all banks and financial institutions will be closed until further notice.

This is the only kind of fiat drastic reform than can get the Federal Reserve, the banks, and the overspent government off the financial hook they have spent themselves onto.

Certainly there will be financial panic, but not among the financial insiders who knew all along it was coming. They will be well prepared to ride out the storm, while the rest of us do the best we can to survive until the "new money" becomes available to us. To participate in the new money, we will be eternally in debt to the financial interests and their government bureaucrats, well into future generations. We will have to turn in all our gold, if we own any, and all our "old money" in our savings and checking accounts and investments in order to be issued "new money" in whatever value the financial masters see fit to redeem it for the old, that is, the current worthless paper we now use as currency.

Such a scenario would require an automatic "temporary" suspension of Constitutional rights until the "financial crisis" was over, however long that might be.

The temporary suspension of Constitutional rights would mean the suspension of liberty, of freedom, of human rights and, possibly, even spiritual rights.

Would this cause a rebellion among the American populace? Not if the financial interests planned and calculated correctly. They would have judged the reluctance for sound money reform and deduced it might be because of fear. With the moral character of the nation weakened by limitations on prayer and Bible reading in public schools, by the diminished regard for human life and human rights through acceptance of murder by abortion on demand, by acceptance of a drug culture—beginning with marijuana considered a "minor" drug offense and others phased in with time, by deterioration of patriotism, by the tearing down of American heroes, by the destruction of a national purpose with no-win wars and pointless military excursions, by the weakening of the national mind through junk television programming and the weakening of the national physique by junk and harmful food distribution and consumption—by all the things that have gone to change America from the world's most powerful nation to just another country in this century—the powers in this scenario might well have deduced correctly that the Americans would submit to this latest dictatorial order as they have to many previous government and financial rulings they didn't want, and never got to vote on, but somehow accepted anyway.

We don't know that such a thing would happen, and we pray to God it never does, but nothing seems impossible within the realm of this sinful world in which man would rule over God. But if this happens, what should one do or have done, to be prepared?

We offer the following suggestions, for what they are worth, to be prepared for either the transition to a gold standard and sound money or for the government-Federal Reserve seizure of the currency:

1. Owe nothing. Make every effort now to pay all debts and owe no one anything. It may be impossible financially to pay off a house mortgage but a house may be about the only or at least the last money shelter to be taken, especially if the occupant-purchaser has established a good mortgage payment record.

2. Clear all properties. In addition to paying all debts, pay off all loans and any other encumbrances on stocks, bonds, second mortgages, any kind of collateral. The more of your possessions you have under your direct control, the better off you will be in any future financial crisis.

3. Have a thirty-day cash supply on hand, outside the banks or any other financial institutions, to tide you over until some kind of accommodation is made for the crisis. The cash will naturally be in the present form of currency but it will probably suffice for awhile during

an emergency. Gold or silver would have far greater purchasing power than paper currency.

4. Get rid of all credit cards and any bills owed to them.

5. Have at least a 90 to 120 day supply of staples on hand—dried and canned foods, flour, sugar, salt, a supply of water. Control of utilities—electricity, heating oil or natural gas, water—might be expected to coerce rebellious elements of the populace into submission to the new monetary regime.

Such precautions may not be enough to allow one to hold out indefinitely in such a scenario, but it could get a household through the immediate crisis. And such precautions, if they can be afforded, might be handy to have almost anytime and certainly would be prudent financially if they could be implemented.

This scenario and the precautions to meet it are outlined merely to illustrate that a transitional reform to gold and sound money would not be as difficult as some might have us believe and certainly nowhere as hard as the ''new money'' scenario.

Gold has widely-known qualities that far outshine and outweigh paper. It has been recognized as a commodity of value since early Biblical times.

''And the gold of that land is good: there is bdellium and the onyx stone.''—Genesis 2:12.

Gold is the most imperishable and stable of the metallic elements. It does not tarnish, rust or corrode. It is the most easily worked and fabricated of all metals. It is dense, nineteen times heavier than water. Gold is easily divisible and portable. Its value is recognized world-wide and is acceptable as a medium of exchange in all places and all ages.

Gold has always been the world's best money; but, as every Christian knows from experience, faith in Christ and prayer are more powerful and more valuable than gold. So far as this sinful world is concerned, gold is the best commodity, the best money. But, so far as the heavenly kingdom of Jesus Christ is concerned, all the worry and concern and greed for gold or what it will buy is unimportant.

''Neither their silver nor their gold shall be able to deliver them in the day of the Lord's wrath...''—Zephaniah 1:18.

''Then Peter said, 'silver and gold have I none; but such as I have give I thee: In the name of Jesus Christ of Nazareth rise up and walk.'''—Acts 3:6.

No matter what earthly preparations we have made or precautions we have taken, now is the time to rise up and walk with Jesus Christ. He is coming to take out of this world all born-again believers. While we live here on this earth, we may as well be prepared to meet its trials and tribulations, but most important is to be prepared to meet Jesus when He returns. Without that preparation, all others are useless, anyway.

FOOTNOTES

Chapter 1

Power of the Pursestring

[1] Billy James Hargis, "The Great Fort Knox Gold Scandal," *Christian Crusade Newspaper*, January, 1983, p. 1.

[2] *Ibid.*, p. 2.

[3] F. P. Walters, *A History of the League of Nations* (London: Oxford University Press, 1965), pp. 89, 111-112, 291, 357-358, 416.

[4] Raymond L. Buell, *Europe: A History of Ten Years* (New York, The Macmillan Co., 1928) pp. 78-96. Also see G. P. Auld, *The Dawes Plan and the New Economics* (New York: Doubleday, 1927); C. Bergman, *The History of Reparations* (London: Beun Co., 1925); R. C. Davis, *The Dawes Plan in the Making* (Indianapolis: Bobbs-Merrill, 1925); A. G. Moulton and Leonid Pasvolsky, *World War Debt Settlements* (New York: The Macmillan Co., 1924), "Reparation Documents", pp. 145-218; Economic Subcommittee on Reparations, The League of Nations, *The Experts' Plan for Reparations Payments* (Paris: League of Nations Reparations Commission, 1926).

[5] Edward J. Epstein, "Ruling the World of Money," *Harper's Magazine*, November, 1983, pp. 43-44.

[6] Anthony Sampson, *The Money Lenders—Bankers and a World in Turmoil* (New York: The Viking Press, 1981), p. 65.

[7]. Epstein, "Ruling the World of Money," p. 44.

[8]. Billy James Hargis and Bill Sampson, "An Armand Hammer Update: The Rape of Cities Service Shocks Oil, Finance Circles," *Christian Crusade Newspaper*, November, 1983, pp. 14-15.

[9]. Randolph E. Paul, *Taxation in the United States* (New York: Little, Brown and Co., 1964), p. 326 ff.

[10] *Ibid.*

[11] Epstein, "Ruling the World of Money," pp. 47-48.

[12] Anthony Sutton and Patrick Wood, *Trilaterals Over Washington* (Scottsdale, Ariz.: The August Corp., 1978, 1981), 2 vols.; John E. McManus, *The Insiders: A Look at the Powerful Men Who Dictate American Policy* (Belmont, Mass.: The John Birch Society, 1979), pp. 9-13, 19-21; Dan Smoot, *The Invisible Government* (Dallas: The Dan Smoot Report, 1978); Richard Harvey, "Trilateralists are Running America," *The Texas Tribune*, Feb. 28, 1980, p. 4; Taylor Gray, "Goldwater Assails Trilateral Control of White House," *The Spotlight*, Feb. 11, 1980, p. 14; Johnny Stewart, *Will Rockefeller's One-Worlders Bankrupt Us?* (Waco, Texas: Fund to Restore an Educated Electorate, 1978), pp. 1-4 (pamphlet); Phoebe Courtney, *What the Nation's Press Isn't Telling You About the Trilateral Commission* (Littleton, Colo.: The Independent American, 1980), pp. 1-6 (pamphlet); no author, *The Council on Foreign Relations-Trilateral Commission Puppet Show* (Glendale, Calif.: Community Churches of America, 1980), pp. 1-8 (pamphlet); n.a., "The Trilateral List," *The Review of the News*, March 16, 1977, pp. 39-40, and many other sources on the topic.

[13] Bill Moyers, "The World of David Rockefeller," *Bill Moyers' Journal* (transcript, television broadcast, Public Television Stations: originated on WNET, Boston), Feb. 7, 1980.

[14] *Ibid.*

[15] *Ibid.*

[16] *Ibid.*

[17] Billy James Hargis and Bill Sampson, "Slave Labor Report: Women, Children Work on Soviet Pipeline," *Christian Crusade Newspaper*, January, 1983, p. 4.

[18] George Will, "Officials Ignore Anti-Slave Labor Law," *Tulsa World*, Nov. 29, 1983, p. 10 A.

[19⁰] Epstein, "Ruling the World of Money," pp. 44-45.

[20] *Ibid.*, p. 45.

Chapter 2

The Federal Reserve:
The Cradle of Communism and Other Conspiracies

[1] Eustace Mullins, *The Federal Reserve Conspiracy* (Hawthorne, Calif.: Omni Publications, 1971), pp. 69-71.

[2] Count Egon Caesar Conti, *The Rise of the House of Rothschild* (Belmont, Mass.: Western Islands, reprint of 1928 Cosmopolitan Book Corp., 1972), pp. 107 ff.

[3] Billy James Hargis and Bill Sampson, "Who Owns the Federal Reserve?," *Christian Crusade Newspaper*, September, 1983, p. 15; Jim Townsend, "Court Says Fed is Privately Owned," *The Spotlight*, Jan. 17, 1983; Col. Archibald Roberts, "Elite Club Owns the Fed," *The*

Spotlight, Dec. 27, 1982, p. 2.

[4] 425 *U.S.* 807; 96 *Sup Ct.* 1971; 48 *L. Ed. 2d* 390 (1976).

[5] U.S., *House Report No. 69*, 63rd Congress, 1st sess., pp. 18-19 (1913).

[6] 12 *U.S.C.* 30.

[7] 12 *U.S.C.* 341-361.

[8] Dorothy M. Nichols, *Modern Money Mechanics—A Workbook on Deposits, Currency and Bank Reserves* (Chicago: Federal Reserve Bank of Chicago, 1961, revised 1968, 1971, 1975, 1982), p. 3.

[9] Patman is quoted in Gary Allen, "Federal Reserve: The Trillion Dollar Conspiracy," *American Opinion Magazine*, February, 1976, p. 8.

[10] Mullins, *The Federal Reserve Conspiracy*, pp. 68-69. Also see Gary Allen, *None Dare Call It Conspiracy* Seal Beach, Calif.: Concord Press, 1971); Gary Allen, *The Rockefeller File* (Seal Beach, Calif.: '76 Presss, 1976), pp. 102-107; Anthony Sutton, *Wall Street and the Bolshevik Revolution* (New Rochelle, N.Y.: Arlington House, 1975).

[11] U.S., Department of the Treasury, "Statement of the U.S. Treasury on Consolidation of Gold Accounts Administered by the Treasury," *Treasury Department New Release*, Washington D.C., Dec. 9, 1974, p. 1; Edward Durell, *Mr. President, Where is Our Gold?* (Berryhill, Va.: privately printed report of Dr. Franz Pick's seminar, New York City, June 29-30, 1981), pp. 1-5 ff.

[12] Malcolm Windust, "The Communist Trusts in Russia," *Fortnightly Magazine* (London), July, 1922, p. 1 ff.

[13] Mullins, *The Federal Reserve Conspiracy*, p. 106.

[14] Ross M. Robertson, *History of the American Economy* (New York: Harcourt, Brace, Jovanovich, 1973), 3d. ed., pp. 161-198, 402-438.

[15] Charles P. Kindleberger, *Mania, Panics and Crashes: A History of Financial Crises* (New York: Basic Books, Inc., 1978), p. 5.

[16] Marcia Stigum, *The Money Market* (Homewood, Ill.: Dow Jones-Irwin, 1983), rev. ed., pp. 123-125, 324-326.

[17] Eugene L. Barker, William E. Dodd and Walter P. Webb, *The Growth of a Nation* (Evanston, Ill.: Row, Peterson and Co., 1928, 1934), pp. 672, 677, 707.

[18] Charles and Mary Beard, *History of the United States: A Study in American Civilization* (New York: The Macmillan Co., 1945), pp. 612-613, 666.

[19] Barker, Dodd and Webb *The Growth of a Nation*, p. 677.

[20] Board of Governors of the Federal Reserve System, *Welcome to the Federal Reserve* (Washington: Federal Reserve, 1980), pamphlet, p. 2.

[21] *Ibid.*, p. 1.

[22] *Ibid.*, pp. 9-10.

[23] Mullins, *The Federal Reserve Conspiracy*, pp. 1-25.

[24] Robertson, *History of the American Economy*, p. 436.

[25] *New York Times*, March 24, 1910, p. 1.

[26] Mullins,m *The Federal Reserve Conspiracy*, pp. 1-25.

[27] Ely Garrison, *Roosevelt, Wilson and The Federal Reserve Act* (New York: n.p., 1915), p. 145.

[28] Allen, "Federal Reserve: The Trillion Dollar Conspiracy," p. 9.

[29] Milton Friedman, "More Double Talk at the Fed," *Newsweek*, May 2, 1983, p. 72.

[30] Rep. Ron Paul and Lewis Lehrman, *The Case for Gold, A Minority Report of the U.S. Gold Commission* (Washington: Cato Institute, 1982), i.

[31] John M. Berry, "The Money Supply Issue: The Treasury is Again at Odds with the Fed," *The Washington Post National Weekly Edition*, Dec. 12, 1983, pp. 18-19.

[32] *Ibid.*

[33] *Ibid.*

[34] *Ibid.*

[35] Robert J. Samuelson, "Money and Myth: The Presumed Independence of the Fed," *The Washington Post National Weekly Edition*, Dec. 5, 1983, p. 34, a review of Maxwell Newton's, *The Fed: Inside the Federal Reserve, the Secret Power That Controls the American Economy* (New York: Time Books, 1983).

[36] U.S., *House Report No. 1635*, 70th Congress, 2d sess. (1931).

[37] David Halberstam, *The Power That Be* New York: Alfred A. Knopf, 1979), p. 713, also pp. 160, 178-180, 190-192, 311-312, 710-711.

Chapter 3

Fed Confetti: Funny, Phony Money

[1] n.a., "Yap Island Money Always Good," *Life Magazine*, April 25, 1949, p. 100.

[2] Ryan C. Amacher, *Principles of Economics* (Cincinnati: South-Western Publishing Co., 1983), pp. 56-64.

[3] Nichols, *Modern Money Mechanics*, p. 2.

[4] Associated Press, "Dollar Soars to Record Highs Against Major World Currencies," *Tulsa World*, Dec. 6, 1983, p. 8 B.

[5] Adam Smith, *Paper Money* (New York: Summit Books, 1981), pp. 114-117.

[6] U.S., Senate, 81st Congress, 1st sess., Senate Internal Security Subcommittee Report, *Interlocking Subversion in Government Departments*, July 30, 1952, p. 29; U.S., Senate, 78th Congress, 1st sess., *Hearings on Occupation Currency Transaction*, Senate Appropriations, Armed Services and Banking Committees, 1947, pp. 8, 27, 175-179; John A. Stormer, *None Dare Call It Treason* (Florissant, Mo.: Liberty Bell Press, 1965), p. 29.

[7] Sampson, *The Money Lenders*, p. 67.

8 Thomas G. Evans, *The Currency Carousel, A New Era in Monetary Affairs* (Princeton: Dow Jones Books, 1977), pp. 4-5.

9 Smith, *Paper Money*, pp. 122-124.

10 *Ibid.*, p. 125.

11 *Ibid.*, pp. 66-89.

12 Elbert V. Bowden, Principles of Economics (Cincinnati: South-Western Books, 1983), pp. 107-108.

13 *Ibid.*, pp. 127-133.

14 Irwin A. Schiff, *The Biggest Con: How the Government is Fleecing You* (Hamden, Conn.: Freedom Books, 1977), p. 21.

15 645, 62 *U.S. Statutes* 749 (1948).

16 Schiff, *The Biggest Con*, pp. 22-28.

17 8 Wall 625.

18 110 *U.S.* 421, *Julliard v. Greenman*, (1884).

19 Bismarck in quoted in Gertrude M. Cougan, *Money Creators* (Hawthorne, Calif.: Omni Publications, 1935), p. 216.

20 n.a., "The Red Dollar," *Tulsa World*, Dec. 13, 1983, p. 6 B.

21 Phoebe Courtney, *Why the Coming "Cashless" Society?* (Littleton, Colo.: The Independent American, 1982), pamphlet, pp. 5-8.

22 Andrea L. Coccia and Patricia M. Scherschel, "Time to Throw Away Your Checkbook?," *U.S. News and World Report*, Dec. 5, 1983, pp. 86-87.

23 Mary Stewart Relfe, *When Your Money—The 666 System is Here* (Montgomery, Ala.: Ministries, Inc., 1981), p. 238.

24 Doug Clark, *The End of Your Money—The Death of the Dollar* (Orange, Calif.: Amazing Prophecy Center, 1973), p. 45. Also see Doug Clark, *100 Hidden Facts About Your Money* (Orange: Amazing Prophecy Center, 1974).

25 Stanley N. Wellborn, "Machines That Think," *U.S. News and World Report*, Dec. 5, 1983, pp. 59-62.

26 Ludwig Von Mises, translated from German by H.E. Batson, *The Theory of Money and Credit* (Indianapolis: Liberty Classics, 1981), p. 454. The original edition was published in 1912 and was revised through 1954 by Dr. Von Mises.

27 *Ibid.*, pp. 454-459.

28 W. Cleon Skousen, *The Urgent Need for a Comprehensive Monetary Reform* (Salt Lake City: The Freeman Institute, 1982), pp. 1, 16-18.

29 Ron Paul, "The Monetary Freedom Act," *Congressional Record*, March 24, 1983, E 1306-1307.

30 Alexander Hamilton, John Jay, James Madison, ed. Clinton Rossiter, *The Federalist Papers* (New York: Mentor Books, 1961), p. 283.

31 Bill Sampson, excerpts from a speech, "The Twilight of Money," *Christian Crusade Bible Conference for God and Country*, Neosho, Mo., Oct. 19, 1983.

[32] Cathy Milam, "For Richer or Pooer—Three Generations of Money," *Tulsa World*, Dec. 11, 1983, p. 1 F.

[33] Von Mises, *The Theory of Money and Credit*, pp. 251, 261.

[34] Paul and Lehrman, *The Case for Gold*, i.

Chapter 4
Capitalists and Communists:
The Perverted Partnership

[1] There is considerable scholarly and popular evidence to support this statement, but much of it has been ignored by conventional news media, academics and publishing houses. See Anthony Sutton, *Western Technology and Soviet Economic Development* (New Rochelle, N.Y.: Arlington House, 1977), 3 vols.; Anthony Sutton, *Wall Street and the Bolshevik Revolution* (New Rochelle: Arlington House, 1975); Senator William Armstrong, "The Leakage of Western Technology," *Congressional Record*, April 18, 1983, S 4818-4821; Admiral James D. Watkins, "Technology Transfer—A Costly Race With Ourselves," a speech to the *Navy League* luncheon, Pasadena, Calif., Jan. 3, 1983; General Charles Gabrield, "Technology Holds the Key," a speech to the *Air Force Association* convention, Washington, D.C., Aug. 5, 1982; footnote 12, Chapter 1 and footnote 6, Chapter 3 of this book.

[2] Joseph Finder, "Dr. Armand Hammer's Medicine Show—How to Parlay One Hour With Lenin Into a Capitalist Empire," *Harper's Magazine*, July, 1983, pp. 30-42; Hargis and Sampson, "The Rape of Cities Service," *Christian Crusade Newspaper*, November, 1983 pp. 14-15.

[3] Allen, *The Rockefeller File*, p. 107.

[4] U.S., War Department, "The Influence of General Phillip R. Faymonville on Soviet-American Relations," *General Staff Report*, located in the private papers of Maj. Gen. Edwin Watson, military aide to President Franklin D. Roosevelt, manuscript department, University of Virginia Library, Accession No. 9786, Box 29, marked "Intelligence Folder," circa 1934-1935.

[5] Allen, *The Rockefeller File*, p. 109.

[6] John Franklin Carter, writing under the pseudonym "The Unofficial Observer," *Our Lords and Masters—Known and Unknown Rulers of the World* (New York: Simon and Schuster, 1935), pp. 220-221. Also see Robert Payne, *The Life and Death of Adolf Hitler* (New York: Popular Library, 1973), pp. 213, 253 and Joseph Borkin, *The Crime and Punishment of I.G. Farben* (New York: Pocket Books, 1978), pp. 53, 71, 78-80, 91, 171.

[7] Smith, *Paper Money*, p. 57.

[8] *Ibid.*, pp. 58-60.

[9] Carter, *Our Lords and Masters*, pp. 221-223.

[10] *Ibid.*, pp. 224-226.

[11] Von Mises, *The Theory of Money and Credit*, pp. 296-297.

[12] Carol S. Greenwald, *Banks Are Dangerous to Your Wealth* (Englewood Cliffs, N.J.: Prentice-Hall, 1980), p. 57.

[13] Martin Mayer, *The Bankers* (New York: Weybright and Talley, 1974), p. 112.

[14] Peter Collier and David Horowitz, *The Rockefellers—An American Dynasty* (New York: Holt, Rinehart and Winston, 1976), pp. 310-323, 405-433, 521-525,m 560-561.

[15] Sampson, *The Money Lender*, p. 80.

[16] *Ibid.*, p. 81.

[17] Allen, *The Rockefeller File*, p. 30.

[18] *Ibid.*, pp. 31-32.

[19] Sampson, The Money Lender, pp. 268-279.

[20] Robert F. Black and Patricia Scherschel, "Bankers: Everybody's Favorite Target," *U.S. News and World Report*, April 11, 1983, p. 27.

[21] *Ibid.*

[22] Thomas Sowell, "Second Thoughts About the Third World," *Harper's Magazine*, November, 1983, pp. 33-42.

[23] *Ibid.*, p. 42.

[24] Robert J. McCartney, "Turning the Corner in Mexico," *The Washington Post National Weekly Edition*, Nov. 28, 1983, p. 23.

[25] Robert M. Bartell, " 'Radical' Victory in Argentian Means Banksters Are Boss," *The Spotlight*, Nov. 14, 1983, p. 1.

[26] Senator John Melcher, "Senate Debate on Amendment No. 1256, Budget Reduction," *Congressional Record*, May 11, 1983, S 6482.

[27] n.a., "Report No. 25," *Sharing International Responsibilities* (New York: Trilateral Commission, 1982), p. 6.

[28] *Washington Times*, May 4, 1983.

[29] *The New York Times*, June 17, 1983.

[30] *Ibid.*

[31] *Washington Times*, Jan. 21, 1983.

[32] C. B. Baker, "The Bankers' War Against America," *Youth Action News*, July, 1983, p. 7.

[33] David Fairlamb and Henriette Sender, "Rescuing the Banking System," *Dun's Business Monthly*, February, 1983, p. 50.

[34] Henry Hazlitt, *Economics in One Lesson* (New York: Manor Books, 1962), p. 12.

[35] *Ibid.*

Chapter 5

You Can Bank On This

[1] Gordon Williams, *Financial Survival in the Age of New Money* (New York: Simon and Schuster, 1981), pp. 143-145.

[2] Elbert V. Bowden, *Revolution in Banking: Regulatory Changes, the*

New Competitive Environment and the "New World" for the Financial Services Industry in the 1980s (Richmond, Va.: Robert F. Dame, Inc., 1980), p. 128.

[3] Greenwald, *Banks Are Dangerous to Your Wealth*, p. 226.

[4] James L. Rowe Jr., "A Turf Battle Among the Regulators," *The Washington Post National Weekly Edition*, Dec. 19, 1983, p. 19.

[5] Jay Palmer, "The Debt Bomb," *Time Magazine*, Jan. 10, 1983, p. 44.

[6] *Ibid.*

[7] Paul and Lehrman, *The Case for Gold*, pp. 192-193.